LOUISIANA
Hometown Cookbook

LOUISIANA
Hometown Cookbook

by Sheila Simmons and Kent Whitaker

Great American Publishers
www.GreatAmericanPublishers.com
toll-free 1.888.854.5954

Recipe Collection © 2010 by Great American Publishers

Great American Publishers

P. O. Box 1305 ✦ Kosciusko, MS 39090
TOLL-FREE 1.888.854.5954 ✦ www.GreatAmericanPublishers.com

ISBN 978-1-934817-07-0

10 9 8 7 6 5 4 3

by Sheila Simmons & Kent Whitaker

Front cover photos: Louisiana Plantation © J.P. Gisclair; Jesters © Vicenc Feliu bigstockphoto.com;
Cypress © Richard Hoffkins bigstockphoto.com; Gumbo © StockFood/Dennis Gottlieb

Back cover photos: Bread Pudding © Josh Monken; Gator © Evelyn White, Stark Mayhaw Festival

Chapter opening photos: istockphoto.com: Appetizers p9 © Dragan Trifunovic ✦ Breads p27 © Thomas
Perkins ✦ Salads p51 © Kelly Cline ✦ Vegetables p105 © Diane Diederich ✦ Meat p129 © Carol Gering ✦
Fish p179 © Suzanne Tucker ✦ Cookies p217 © Jim Jurica ✦ shutterstock.com: Soups p73 © Thomas M.
Perkins ✦ Pies p243 © Giordano Borghi ✦ Index p245 © Angel Davis.

CONTENTS

6·

INTRODUCTION

Louisiana and Good Food... the two are synonymous. From world-renowned restaurants to skilled hometown cooks there is great food around every corner of the state, and food here is as much about heritage as sustenance.

Every day is a party in Louisiana. From local music to zoos and museums, from street performers to fishing on the bayou, from Mardi Gras celebrations to quiet strolls through centuries-old plantation homes, there is something for every one to enjoy in the Pelican State.

Classic Louisiana cooking is about cooking for friends and family. Here, you find many classic dishes like *Beignets*, *Seafood Gumbo*, *King Cake*, *Shrimp Etouffée*, and *Alligator Stew* from South Louisiana. And from North Louisiana, there are favorites like *Old-Fashioned Buttermilk Biscuits*, Hot Sausage Black-Eyed Pea Casserole, and *Collard Greens*. You will find new creations... *Crawfish Cakes with Creollaise Sauce*, *Holy Trinity Mardi Gras Potatoes*, and *Party Pecan Rum Cake*... And traditional dishes... *New Orleans Bread Pudding*, *Grits and Grillades*, *Corn Maque Choux*, and *Bananas Foster*... Not to mention, *Crab Stuffed Deviled Eggs*, *Cajun Beer Bread*, *Grannies Hot Crockpot Candy*, and *Grilled Fish Orleans*.

Louisiana's unique architecture, lively music, and delicious food all come together during the many festivals that are held throughout the state each year. And throughout this book, you'll find informative stories about fun, food-related festivals. From **Louisiana Oyster Jubilee** in New Orleans to the **Zwolle Tamale Festival**, from **Mudbug Madness** in Shreveport to Abbeville's **Giant Omelette Celebration**, Starks **Mayhaw Festival** to Mandeville **Seafood Festival**, Ponchatoula's **Strawberry Festival** to Ruston's **Squire Creek Louisiana Peach Festival**, there is a celebration to suit every taste.

Louisiana lives by the phrase, "laissez les bon temps rouler." And it's easy to Let the Good Times Roll at Louisiana's many many festivals, all of which are listed on page 254.

This, the fourth volume in our State Hometown Cookbook Series, would not be possible without the generous support of many people. Kent and I spoke to numerous people throughout the state who generously shared their recipes, their stories, and their memories. Thank you to everyone associated with the food festivals, Chambers of Commerce, and tourist bureaus who were ever patient and helpful.

Our sincere gratitude goes to Leslie Shoemaker, Brooke Craig, and Anita Musgrove who are forever working tirelessly behind the scenes, and to the best Hometown Sales Team around: Angel Franklin, Krista Griffin, Jenny Harrell, Ashley Richmond, Tabitha Medders, and Sheree Adcox. A very special thank you goes to Gwen McKee who instilled in me a love of Louisiana food, training in the art of cookbook making, and more than 18 years of friendship. And, as always, a big thank you goes to our families for their unwavering support; Ally and Macee, Roger, Ryan, and Nicholas—we couldn't do it without you.

Louisiana Hometown Cookbook is for Louisiana residents, visitors, transplanted natives or anyone who wants to experience the unique flavor of the state's special food heritage. We hope you will enjoy this outstanding collection of the best recipes from hometown cooks across the state.

Wishing you many happy kitchen memories,

Sheila Simmons & Kent Whitaker

Beverages & Appetizers

Bayou Mary

4 ounces tomato juice
2 tablespoons lemon or lime juice
1 teaspoon Worcestershire Sauce
Dash salt and pepper
1 teaspoon hot sauce

Combine and shake. Serve over ice garnished with celery, if desired.

Cranberry Collins

3 cups cranberry juice
1 cup lemon or lime juice
½ cup club soda
Ice
Lime Slices

Mix cranberry juice, lemon or lime juice, and club soda well; serve over ice with a lime as garnish.

Kathleen's "Knock You Naked" Margaritas

1 lime
1 small can lime-aid
1 can tequila (using lime-aid can for measuring)
½ can triple sec (using lime-aid can for measuring)
½ can white wine (using lime-aid can for measuring)
Splash lime juice
Ice
Margarita Salt

Guaranteed for a great "Girls weekend" at the beach.

Cut lime in half; cut rind away. Place ½ lime in blender, pulp and all. Add liquid ingredients; add ice to the top. Blend until smooth. Salt glasses by rubbing lime on rims, then dip in salt. Serve immediately.

Kathleen Robinson from the "Robinson & Stirling Family Recipe Collection"

THE PLAQUEMINES PARISH FAIR & ORANGE FESTIVAL

First Full Weekend in December • Belle Chasse

Taste a slice of Louisiana at the Plaquemines Parish Fair & Orange Festival. Each year, thousands of visitors come to Plaquemine Parish to experience one of the oldest and most unique Festivals in the State of Louisiana. Come help us celebrate the Citrus Industry and the people behind it with fun activities for the entire family. You will experience wonderful food, entertainment, contests, crafts, novelties, and hospitality. Join for Louisiana's favorite festival with Orange-A-Peel.

504.656.7599 • www.orangefestival.com

Punch

½ cup lemon juice
2 quarts cranberry juice
3 cups orange juice
3 cups pineapple juice
1 liter ginger ale, chilled
1 orange, sliced

Combine all ingredients, except sliced orange, in a container and chill. Serve over ice with an orange slice as garnish.

Orange Lime Smoothie

1 can cream of coconut
3 cups orange juice
Juice of 1 lime or lemon
1 scoop vanilla ice cream
1½ cups ice
Dash nutmeg

Mix all ingredients, except nutmeg, in a blender until smooth. Sprinkle with nutmeg.

Miss Vivian's Spiced Tea

Spices:

2 whole nutmeg
3 cinnamon sticks
1 tablespoon whole cloves
1 tablespoon whole allspice

Tea:

5 tea bags
½ cup sugar
1 can orange juice concentrate
1 can lemonade concentrate
2 small cans pineapple juice (about 1½ cups)
2 small cans apple juice (about 1½ cups)

Vivian Jorgensen was a very close family friend, like an adopted mother. She and her husband, Earl, even traveled with us on family vacations. They had no children of their own and spent every holiday with us.

Boil Spices in 1½ cups water until fragrant. At the same time, boil a pot of strong tea using 5 tea bags in 1½ quarts water. In a large pot or crockpot, combine tea (remove tea bags), sugar, orange juice, lemonade, pineapple juice and apple juice; cook over low heat for several hours. Strain spice water and add to tea. Serve warm or chilled.

Amy Kirsch, Baton Rouge

Honey Apple Tea

4 tea bags
3 cups water, boiling
⅓ cup honey
3 cups apple juice

Steep tea bags in boiling water for 5 minutes. Remove tea bags and mix cooked tea with remaining ingredients. Chill and serve over ice.

Juiced Up Tea

2 quarts iced tea
1 can frozen cranberry juice concentrate
2 cups orange juice
1 cup water
⅓ cup sugar

Combine all and stir until sugar is dissolved. Serve chilled over ice.

Charlie Tucker

Billie Hays' Cheese Ball

2 (8-ounce) packages cream
    cheese, softened
5 ounces Kraft sharp cheese, shredded (about 1¼ cups)
1 tablespoon minced onion
1 tablespoon minced green pepper
1 tablespoon pimento
2 tablespoons Worcestershire Sauce
Dash salt
Dash cayenne
Chopped pecans (or parsley)

Combine all ingredients, except pecans, and form into a ball; chill. Remove from refrigerator, form again into a ball, and roll in chopped pecans or parsley. Serve immediately or refrigerate until ready to serve.

Kathleen Robinson from the "Robinson & Stirling Family Recipe Collection"

Creole Stuffed Brie

1 (8-inch) wheel Brie
¼ cup chopped parsley
1 small clove garlic, minced
1 teaspoon rosemary
1 teaspoon thyme
1 teaspoon hot sauce
1 teaspoon marjoram
⅓ cup cooked crumbled andouille sausage
1 sheet frozen puff pastry, thawed
1 egg, lightly beaten

Chill Brie to harden. Slice Brie in half lengthwise like a bun (chill again if it begins to soften). In a bowl combine parsley, garlic, rosemary, thyme, hot sauce and marjoram. Stir cooked and crumbled sausage into herb mix. Spread mixture over ½ of Brie and press halves back together. Roll pastry to twice the size of Brie. Place Brie in center of rolled pastry. Bring edges of pastry over top and press together using some beaten egg to seal. Place Brie seam-side-down on lightly greased pan. Brush with remaining egg and poke 4 to 5 times with a fork or knife to vent. Bake 30 minutes at 350° or until pastry is golden and puffed. Allow to rest 10 minutes before serving with crackers etc.

ANDOUILLE FESTIVAL

October • LaPlace

Come and celebrate a good time in LaPlace, Louisiana where we honor the best-tasting Andouille sausage in the world. There are lots of bands that play throughout the weekend, down-home cooking sold at the food booths, beautiful crafts, and let's not forget the rides. We have our gumbo cook-off on Saturday and our annual 5-mile Andouille Run on Sunday. So come on over and let us show you a Smokin' Good Time.

985.652.9569 • www.andouillefestival.com

Muffa Pinwheels

3 slices ham
3 slices pepperoni
3 slices salami
3 large flour tortillas
3 ounces cream cheese, softened

¼ cup minced onions
¼ cup chopped mushrooms
¼ cup chopped olives
1 tablespoon hot sauce
½ tablespoon Cajun seasoning

Lay one slice of each meat evenly on tortilla shells. Combine cream cheese, onions, mushrooms, olives, hot sauce and Cajun seasoning in a bowl and mix well. Spread evenly and equally over tortillas and meat; roll up. Chill; when stiff, cut evenly into slices.

Angie Pentier

Crab Stuffed Deviled Eggs

12 large eggs
1 cup cooked and flaked lump crab meat
1 cup mayonnaise
½ tablespoon Old Bay seasoning
1 teaspoon vinegar
½ tablespoon Worcestershire sauce
⅓ cup minced celery
1 teaspoon garlic powder
2 teaspoons hot sauce
Paprika or bacon bits (optional)

This recipe is equally delicious with shrimp crawdad meat substituted for the crab meat.

Boil the eggs; cool, peel and cut in half. Remove egg yolks into a bowl and place egg whites on a serving tray. Combine egg yolks with remaining ingredients. Spoon equal portions into egg white halves; chill. Serve topped with paprika or bacon bits, if desired.

Cream Cheese Shrimp Bites

1 cup minced salad shrimp
1 (8-ounce) package cream cheese, softened
¼ cup milk
¼ cup finely chopped celery
1 tablespoon lime juice
2 teaspoons hot sauce
1 clove garlic, chopped
⅛ teaspoon salt
¼ teaspoon pepper
Melba toast for serving

Combine all ingredients, except Melba toast, in a bowl; mix well. Chill to thicken. Spread equal portions on Melba toast slices. Serve open-faced on a tray.

Charlie Tucker

Shrimp Cocktail

12 medium shrimp,
    peeled and deveined
Juice of ½ lemon
1 teaspoon horseradish
1 teaspoon vinegar
1 teaspoon hot sauce
3 tablespoons ketchup

Place shrimp in individual serving dishes. Combine remaining ingredients and serve on the side for dipping.

Crawfish Cakes with Creollaise Sauce

Crawfish Cakes:

2 pounds crawfish tails, cooked
1 stick butter
1 onion, chopped
2 ribs celery, chopped
1 bell pepper, chopped
1 cup chopped green onions
2 cloves garlic, minced
3 cups Italian breadcrumbs
2 tablespoons lemon juice
1 cup chopped fresh parsley
½ teaspoon each salt, pepper, cayenne, Italian seasoning, garlic powder, and onion powder
2 large eggs, beaten
Flour
¼ cup oil

Roughly chop crawfish and set aside. Sauté vegetables in butter over medium-high until soft. Add crawfish, breadcrumbs, lemon juice, parsley, and seasonings. Cook on low 5 to 7 minutes. Remove from heat; cool. Add beaten eggs; mix well. Shape into patties and lightly dust with a little flour. Heat oil and fry Crawfish Cakes in single layer batches 2 to 3 minutes on each side over medium heat until golden brown. Drain on paper towels. Can be fried 30 minutes ahead of time and reheated in a 350° oven 5 to 10 minutes. Serve with chilled Creollaise Sauce.

Creollaise Sauce:

1½ cups mayonnaise
½ cup Creole mustard
¼ teaspoon mustard
1 tablespoon Worcestershire sauce
Tabasco, onion powder, and garlic powder to taste
Minced onion, minced garlic, minced capers to taste (optional)

Mix all ingredients well and chill until ready to serve.

Jill Carney, Baton Rouge

Crawdad Puffs

Puff pastry
1 (8-ounce) packages cream cheese, softened
1 cup cooked minced crawfish meat
½ cup mayonnaise
¼ cup sour cream
2 tablespoons minced chives
2 tablespoons diced onion
1 teaspoon spicy mustard
⅛ teaspoon garlic powder
⅓ cup chopped olives

Cut pastry into 2 inch squares. Combine remaining ingredients to make filling. Spoon equal amounts filling into center of each pastry. Fold up and pinch edges. Cook in a mini muffin tin or regular-sized muffin tin treated with nonstick spray. Bake at 375° 25 minutes until golden and puffed.

Ben's Lobster Loaf Dip

5 ounces lobster meat
2 tablespoons margarine
2 cups shredded Cheddar cheese
¼ teaspoon red pepper sauce
⅓ cup dry white wine

I have used lobster, crab, and even crawfish meat for this recipe; all work well. Perfect for parties and tailgating Tiger football.

Coarsely chop lobster and set aside. Melt butter over low heat. Gradually stir in cheese until melted. Add red pepper sauce. Slowly add wine, stirring until mixture is smooth. Add lobster and stir until heated. Serve warm in a hollowed out round bread bowl. Save hollowed out portions for dipping.

Ben & Linda Campbell, LSU Football Fans

Cajun Caviar

3 cans black-eyed peas,
   drained
1 green bell pepper, chopped
1 red bell pepper, chopped
¼ cup finely chopped jalapeno peppers
1 small sweet onion, chopped
1 can whole kernel corn, drained
¼ cup chopped pimento
½ tablespoon minced garlic
⅓ cup red wine vinegar
⅔ cups olive oil
1 tablespoon Dijon mustard
Salt and pepper
½ tablespoon hot sauce

In a large bowl combine all ingredients and refrigerate until ready to serve. Drain if needed and serve with tortilla chips, crackers or French bread pieces.

Dale Harper

BOUDIN COOK-OFF

October • Lafayette

A unique celebration that includes Boudin Sampling, cooking demonstrations, live music plus fun and games for kids and family including a Boudin Toss, Pin the Tail on the Pig, Balloon Artist, and more. Join us for a Boudin Eating Contest, Cochon de Lait (Cajun Pig Roast) and your opportunity to vote in the People's Choice competition. This fun-filled day winds down with an awards presentation. Come early; eat more.

boudincookoff.com

Spinach Artichoke Dip

1 stick margarine
1 small bunch green onions, chopped (or 1 medium onion, finely chopped)
1 can artichoke hearts, drained and chopped
1 box frozen chopped spinach, cooked and well drained
8 ounces cream cheese
8 ounces sour cream
1 teaspoon Worcestershire
2 to 3 drops hot sauce
Garlic powder, onion powder and salt to taste
Splash lemon juice
1 cup Romano cheese, grated (divided)
8 ounces pepper jack, grated (divided)

Melt margarine in skillet; sauté onions in margarine until soft. Combine with remaining ingredients, reserving ½ cup Romano and cup pepper jack cheese. Mix well; refrigerate several hours or overnight. Bake in preheated 350° oven 25 to 30 minutes; top with reserved cheeses and broil until lightly browned, about 3 to 5 minutes. Serve hot with tortillas or crackers for dipping.

Jill Carney, Baton Rouge

Broccoli and Mushroom Dip

1 medium onion, finely chopped
½ pound fresh mushrooms, sliced
½ cup margarine
1 can cream of mushroom soup
2 (10-ounce) packages frozen chopped broccoli, cooked and drained
1 (6-ounce) roll garlic cheese
3 to 4 drops tabasco
2 teaspoons lemon juice
1 teaspoon Worcestershire

Sauté onions and mushrooms in margarine until soft. Stir in soup, broccoli, cheese and seasoning. Cook over low heat until cheese melts. Serve hot in chafing dish with corn chips or crackers.

Jill Carney, Baton Rouge

Hot Shrimp Dip

1 cup sour cream
2 (8-ounce) packages cream cheese
Splash lemon juice
3 cans shrimp (or 1 pound small peeled fresh shrimp)
1 can cream of shrimp soup
1 small onion, minced
⅓ cup chopped parsley
Salt and cayenne pepper to taste

Use mixer to beat sour cream, cream cheese, soup and lemon juice. Fold in remaining ingredients. Refrigerate several hours or overnight to enhance flavor. Heat in chafing dish. Serve with pastry shells or gourmet crackers.

Jill Carney, Baton Rouge

Gator Balls

1 pound alligator
  meat, finely chopped
2 teaspoons lemon pepper
1 egg, beaten
½ teaspoon salt
1 tablespoon finely chopped onion
2 tablespoons finely chopped celery
1 tablespoon finely chopped parsley
2 tablespoons chopped green onions
¼ cup breadcrumbs
Flour to dredge
1 cup cooking oil

Combine all ingredients, except flour and oil. Form into 1-inch balls. Refrigerate 1 hour. Roll each ball in flour to cover thoroughly and fry in cooking oil until brown.

Kyle LaBlanc www.crawdads.net

JIM BOWIE FESTIVAL

September • Vidalia

The Jim Bowie Festival began more than 20 years ago to remember the famous Sandbar Fight that took place not far from the small town of Vidalia in the early 1800's. Today, the event includes the Louisiana State Championship Bowie Barbeque Duel, the Backyard BBQ event that's open to pros and amateurs alike, an arts & crafts show and live entertainment. Historian, author, and actor Jack Edmonson returns each year to lead his costumed group of volunteers through an exciting re-enactment of the Sandbar Fight. The festival is held in September, right on the banks of the Mississippi River.

318.336.8223 • www.vidaliala.com

Gator Bobs with Creole Sauce

1 pound tenderized alligator meat
2 green bell peppers
2 sweet onions
1 can beer
1 pound (about 4 cups) flour
1 tablespoon Cajun seasoning
Creole Sauce:
Mayonnaise
Hot mustard
Honey

Cut alligator, bell pepper, and onions into 2-inch pieces. Thread onto 10-inch wooden skewers broken in half alternating pieces. Pour beer into a bowl and beat until foaming stops. Slowly mix with flour and Cajun seasoning. Dip gator bobs in batter and deep fry in hot oil 2 to 3 minutes or until golden brown. In a bowl, mix equal spoonfuls of mayonnaise and mustard. Stir in desired amount of honey and mix well. Use as a dipping sauce.

Angie Pentier

Cajun Party Meatballs

2 pounds ground beef
½ cup minced onion
⅓ cup minced celery
⅓ cup minced green or red bell pepper
2 tablespoons hot sauce
½ pound andouille sausage, crumbled
1 tablespoon hot mustard
1 egg, beaten
¾ cup dried breadcrumbs
1 tablespoon Cajun seasoning
½ cup shredded pepper jack cheese

Combine all ingredients in a bowl and form into meatball-size portions. Bake in batches at 350° until brown and done. Serve with toothpicks.

LOUISIANA CAJUN FOOD FEST

Last Full Weekend in October • Kaplan

The French Food Festival is hosted annually on the last full weekend in October and features over 20 local specialty dishes. Dancing and music, along with Folklife demonstrations on Saturday and Sunday, offer everyone the chance to learn about Cajun life-ways -- boat building, cooking, music and more. More than just a food festival, the French Food Festival includes an old-fashioned carnival midway, complete with games, rides, and cotton candy.

337.643.2400 • www.kaplanchamber.org

Classic Cajun Boudin

2¾ pounds pork butt,
    cut into chunks
1 pound pork liver, cut into pieces
2 quarts spring water
1 cup chopped onions
½ cup chopped bell pepper
½ cup chopped celery
5 teaspoons Cajun seasoning, divided
2 teaspoons cayenne, divided
1½ teaspoons black pepper, divided
1 cup minced parsley, divided
1¼ cups chopped green onions, divided
6 cups medium-grain rice (cooked)

Put pork butt, pork liver, water, onions, bell peppers, celery, 1 teaspoon Cajun seasoning, ¼ teaspoon cayenne, and ¼ teaspoon black pepper in a large heavy pot. Bring to a boil, reduce heat and simmer about 2 hours. Drain, reserving 2 cups broth. Grind pork mixture together with ½ cup parsley and ½ cup green onions in a meat grinder fitted with a ¼-inch die. Add rice. Add remaining Cajun seasoning, cayenne, black pepper, parsley, and green onions; mix well. Add reserved broth slowly, mixing well. Stuff into sausage casings. Heat in a steamer or rice cooker or heat in oven or on the grill for a crisp casing. Serve warm. Freeze leftovers. Serves approximately 32 people as an appetizer. Also makes a great snack or side dish.

Boudin Cookoff, Lafayette

Bread & Breakfast

Mike's Cheese Bread

1 loaf French bread
2 cups (8 ounces) grated Cheddar cheese
½ cup mayonnaise
3 green onions, finely chopped.
2 teaspoons Worcestershire sauce
Salt, cayenne and garlic powder to taste

Cut French bread in half length-wise; set aside. Combine remaining ingredients and spread on both sides of bread. Cut into 2-inch slices. Bake at 375° for 20 minutes or until cheese is brown and bubbly.

Kathleen Robinson from the "Robinson & Stirling Family Recipe Collection"

Cajun Beer Bread

4 cups self-rising flour
3 teaspoons brown sugar
1 tablespoon minced onion
1 small can green chilies
½ teaspoon honey
2 eggs, beaten
1 can beer

Mix all ingredients well. Place in greased bread pan and bake 55 minutes at about 350°.

Stephen Nash, Baton Rouge

Crawfish Bread

1 teaspoon baking soda
1 ⅓ cups vegetable oil
1 onion, chopped
2 cups (8 ounces) shredded Cheddar cheese
1 cup yellow cornmeal
1 (14- to 15-ounce) can cream-style corn
½ cup chopped jalapeno peppers
1 teaspoon salt
2 pounds Louisiana crawfish tail meat

Preheat oven to 350°. Mix all ingredients, except crawfish, in blender. Puree until blended. Pour into greased oblong pan or 9x12-inch baking dish. Add crawfish to mixture in pan. Stir to distribute crawfish evenly. Bake 35 to 40 minutes. Serves 6 to 8.

Kyle LaBlanc www.crawdads.net

CAJUN MUSIC AND FOOD FESTIVAL
3rd Weekend in July • Lake Charles

Music, food, crafts, folks and fun are what you will find at the Cajun Music and Food Festival. Since the first festival in 1987, it has continued to grow in size and reputation and has been named as a Southeast Tourism Society Top 20 Event. The two-day event features bands, dancing, Cajun dance troupe demonstrations, Cajun Dance contests, heritage displays, lots of Cajun food and crafts. The CFMA Beauty Pageant Competition is held the weekend before the festival on the 2nd Saturday in July.

337.562.9156 • www.cfmalakecharles.org

Crawfish Cornbread

2 cups yellow cornmeal
1 teaspoon baking soda
1 tablespoon salt
6 eggs
2 medium onions, chopped
4 cups (16 ounces) shredded Cheddar cheese
⅔ cup oil
2 (14- to 15-ounce) cans cream-style corn
½ cup sliced jalapeno peppers
2 pounds Louisiana crawfish tail meat

In a large bowl, combine dry ingredients. In a medium bowl beat eggs thoroughly. Add onions, cheese, oil, corn, jalapeno peppers, and crawfish. Add egg mixture to cornmeal mixture; mix well. Bake in a 9x13-inch baking dish for 55 minutes at 375° or until golden brown. Serves 12.

Kyle LaBlanc www.crawdads.net

Louisiana Sweet Tater Pone

4 to 5 sweet potatoes, peeled
1 cup sugar
½ cup butter
½ cup milk
1 teaspoon vanilla
2 tablespoons cinnamon
1 teaspoon allspice
⅓ cup flour
Oil

I have seen my mother cook this in a pie crust as well. She called it Sweet Tater Pie in a crust and a Pone in the skillet. The only difference was the oil in the skillet is not used for the pie.

Boil sweet potatoes until tender; drain. then mash. Add remaining ingredients except flour and oil. Add flour a little at a time. On top of stove, in a large iron skillet, heat cooking oil (enough to cover bottom of skillet) very hot, pour mixture in and bake in oven at 450° for 30 to 40 minutes.

Renee Hebert & Family

Easy Cast-Iron Skillet Bacon Cornbread

2 boxes cornbread muffin mix, plus ingredients
   as directed on box
½ cup bacon bits
3 tablespoons solid vegetable shortening

Preheat oven to 400°.

Mix cornbread per directions on box; add bacon bits. Heat shortening in a large cast-iron skillet over medium-high heat until almost smoking. Pour in batter. Bake at 375° until golden brown.

This is a very simple recipe that tastes like homemade while using boxed cornbread mix. You can also add peppers and onions for added flavor.

Stephen Nash, Baton Rouge

Hush Puppies

1½ cups cornmeal
¾ cup flour
2 teaspoons baking powder
½ teaspoon salt
1 egg, beaten
2 teaspoons minced garlic
1 small onion, finely chopped
1 tablespoon hot sauce
2 teaspoons sugar
Milk
Oil for frying

Combine dry ingredients. Add egg, garlic, onion, hot sauce and sugar; mix well. Add just enough milk to hold mixture together into solid balls. Drop by tablespoonful into deep fryer or deep fat.

Crawfish Puppies

½ cup self-rising flour
1 cup cornmeal
1 onion, finely chopped
1 egg, beaten
1 teaspoon sugar
½ cup minced crawfish meat
Salt, pepper and cayenne pepper to taste
Buttermilk
Vegetable oil

Mix flour, cornmeal, onion, egg, and sugar. Add crawfish and seasoning to taste. Mix with enough buttermilk to make a thick batter. Drop by teaspoonfuls into deep hot oil. Fry until golden brown.

BREAUX BRIDGE CRAWFISH FESTIVAL

First Weekend in May • Breaux Bridge

The Breaux Bridge Crawfish Festival is one of the largest gatherings of world famous Cajun, Zydeco and Swamp Pop musicians with over 30 bands on three stages during the three-day festival. Fun festivities for all ages include a parade, accordion making, Cajun dance and cooking demonstrations, crawfish races, crawfish etouffée cook-off, crawfish eating contest, carnival rides and more. Artists, craftsmen and vendors display their ware for your shopping enjoyment. And, of course, nothing is as unique to Cajuns as eating crawfish and during festival weekend you'll enjoy tasting crawfish prepared in every imaginable way.

337.332.6655 • bbcrawfest.com

Yeast Brunch Rolls

2¼ cups all-purpose flour
3 tablespoons sugar
1 teaspoon salt
1 package dry active yeast
1 egg, beaten
2 large tablespoons shortening
Vegetable oil

Combine flour, sugar and salt; mix well. In a saucepan, bring 1 cup water to a boil, cool slightly, and add yeast. Mix. Add egg and shortening; mix well. Add to dry ingredients and mix well. Form into a ball and rub with oil. Place in a large bowl, cover with plastic wrap and allow to rise until double in size. Break dough into 12 equal pieces, form into balls and place into well-greased muffin pan. Cover very tightly with plastic wrap and allow dough balls to rise again. Bake in a preheated 425° oven about 15 minutes or until rolls are golden brown.

Pecan Monkey Bread

3 cans biscuits cut into fourths
½ cup brown sugar
⅓ cup sugar
½ stick butter, melted
½ cup orange juice
⅔ cup pecans

Gently mix all ingredients without mashing biscuits until everything is evenly coated. Place in a greased bundt pan and bake at 350° for 30 minutes.

Sticky Pecan Crescents

2 cans crescents
¾ cup sugar
1 tablespoon cinnamon
3 tablespoons maple syrup
2 tablespoons butter, melted
1 cup coarsely chopped pecans

Separate crescents and place flat on a cookie sheet. Working quickly, combine remaining ingredients; mix well. Place equal portions into center of each crescent leaving a small amount in the bowl. Roll each crescent up and brush remaining pecan mixture. Bake at 375° until puffed and golden. Serve warm.

ST. RITA PECAN FESTIVAL

Second Full Weekend in November • Harahan

The 17th Annual St. Rita Pecan Festival will boast a wide array of rides, games, food and music. The Top Cats will perform on Friday from 7 to 10 p.m., Bag Of Donuts plays from 7:30 to 10:30 p.m. on Saturday night. On Sunday, Gashouse Gorillaz performs from 2 to 5 p.m. and The Wise Guys from 7 to 10 p.m. Friday, November 13th from 6:00 PM to 12:00 AM (Midnight) Saturday, November 14th from 12:00 PM (noon) to 12:00 AM (Midnight) Sunday, November 15th from 11:00 AM to 11:00 PM

504.733.2915 • stritaharahan.com

Beignets

¼ cup water
2 teaspoons sugar
½ cup evaporated milk
1 package active dry yeast
3½ cups all-purpose flour
1 egg
2 tablespoons lard (shortening)
1 teaspoon salt
½ teaspoon freshly grated nutmeg, optional
Vegetable oil
Powdered sugar

In a medium saucepan over low heat, combine water, 2 teaspoons sugar and evaporated milk; heat to warm (but not hot). Remove from heat and stir in yeast. Let stand 5 to 10 minutes. In a food processor, combine flour, egg, shortening, salt and nutmeg; blend well. Add yeast mixture. Turn blender on and off 4 or 5 times to bring dough together until fairly smooth and non-sticky. If additional flour is needed, add 1 to 2 tablespoons at a time; process just until blended. Place dough on a lightly floured surface; form into a smooth ball. Lightly coat with oil and place in a large bowl. Cover with plastic wrap. Let rise in a warm place until doubled in bulk, about 1½ hours. Punch down dough. Turn out onto a lightly floured surface. Roll out dough into a rectangle about ½ inch thick. Working at a diagonal to rectangle, with a sharp knife, cut dough into 2-inch-wide strips, moving from left to right. Starting at top left and moving toward bottom of rectangle, cut dough diagonally into 2-inch-wide strips to form diamond shapes and place ½ inch apart on ungreased baking sheets. Use all dough, cover and allow to rest and rise about 45 minutes. In a large saucepan with hot oil, cook until brown on both sides. Remove and drain on paper towels. Sift powdered sugar over hot beignets; serve hot.

Bernice Caulter

Bread Pudding

1 loaf French bread
1 cup sugar
1 teaspoon vanilla
4 egg yolks
¼ cup melted butter
8 ounces evaporated milk
2 cups milk

Slice bread into ¼-inch slices and place in baking pan. Place bread slices in the oven for a short time to dry. Mix sugar, vanilla, yolks and butter; stir in both milks. Pour over bread slices. Bake at 450° for about 15 minutes.

Kyle LaBlanc www.crawdads.net

Oak Alley Plantation Vacherie © Jason Major

Oak Alley Plantation
Vacherie

New Orleans Bread Pudding

6 eggs
¾ cup sugar
½ teaspoon cinnamon
½ teaspoon vanilla extract
3 cups heavy cream
6 cups cubed stale bread (if only fresh bread is available,
   dry it in the oven slightly before using)
½ cup raisins, optional

Generously butter an 8- to 10-inch baking pan (8-inch pan will create a thicker bread pudding). In a large mixing bowl, whisk eggs thoroughly. Add sugar and cinnamon and whisk well. Whisk in vanilla and heavy cream. Fold in bread and raisins, and allow to rest 30 minutes. Last 5 minutes of rest time, start oven preheating to 350°. When oven is hot, pour bread mixture into pan. Top with foil and bake 25 minutes. Remove foil and continue to bake until firm and browned on top, about 35 additional minutes. Top with Bourbon Sauce, if desired. Serves 10 to 12.

Bourbon Sauce:

1½ cups heavy cream
1 cup half-and-half
2 teaspoons pure vanilla extract
¼ cup sugar
2 tablespoons cornstarch
3 tablespoons bourbon

Heat cream, half-and-half, vanilla and sugar in a saucepan over high heat, whisking, 3 minutes. Dissolve cornstarch in bourbon. When you see bubbles at edges of cream, whisk in bourbon mixture. Continue to cook and whisk another 2 minutes; when/ if cream boils up like it will overflow pan, remove from heat. Continue to whisk vigorously until sauce begins to thicken. Place over low heat and simmer 1 minute. Sauce will be thin; it is not meant to be very thick. (If you prefer a thicker sauce, add another tablespoon cornstarch.)

Georgia L. Bonin, Sulphur

Old-Fashioned Buttermilk Biscuits

2 cup all-purpose flour, sifted
2 teaspoons baking power
¼ teaspoon baking soda
½ teaspoon salt
4 tablespoons butter
⅓ cup buttermilk

Combine dry ingredients; blend thoroughly. Add butter mixing until mixture resembles coarse crumbs. Add buttermilk a little at a time. Don't overwork the dough. On a floured surface, roll out dough to a circle about ½-inch thick. Cut using a biscuit cutter or glass dipped in flour. Place on a baking sheet and bake at 350° until golden on top and brown on the bottom, about 15 minutes. Serve warm.

Shrimp or Crawdad Biscuit Drops

2¼ cups self-rising flour
¼ cup margarine
½ cup whole milk (more as needed)
Dash salt
Large dash sugar
½ cup minced shrimp or crawfish meat

Combine all ingredients and spoon equal portions onto a greased baking sheet. Bake at 400° until golden. Serve hot. You can add hot sauce and even cheese, if desired.

Hot Ham & Cheese Biscuits

2 cups flour
1 tablespoon baking powder
½ teaspoon salt
½ cup chilled vegetable shortening
¼ cup cold milk
½ cup finely chopped ham
½ cup shredded cheese
1 tablespoon hot sauce, optional

Combine flour, baking powder and salt. Cut in shortening until mixture resembles crumbs. Stir in milk, ham and cheese just until dough holds together. On a floured board knead about 1 minute. With floured rolling pin roll dough ½ inch thick. With floured biscuit cutter cut dough into 2½- to 3-inch rounds. Bake at 400° about 12 to 15 minutes or until lightly browned. Serve hot.

Pain Perdu (Lost Bread)

4 to 6 eggs
3 tablespoons orange-flavored liqueur
2 tablespoons milk
⅓ cup sugar
1 tablespoon lemon zest
12 slices leftover French bread
Oil for skillet
Powdered sugar
Maple syrup

In a medium bowl, combine eggs, liqueur, milk, sugar and lemon zest. Mix until sugar is dissolved. Dip bread slices into batter and coat well. Fry in a skillet with hot oil until golden brown. Drain on paper towels; sprinkle with powdered sugar and serve with hot maple syrup.

Instant Eggs Benedict

Poached Eggs:

Water
½ teaspoon vinegar
8 eggs

In a large saucepan or deep skillet, add water to about 3 inches deep. Bring to a boil then reduce to medium-high. Add ½ teaspoon vinegar. Break eggs and slip into water, one at a time, close to surface of water. Simmer 3 to 5 minutes. Remove with a slotted spoon.

Eggs Benedict:

1 Hollandaise sauce packet
    plus ingredients to prepare per directions
4 English muffins
Butter
8 slices Canadian-style bacon
8 poached eggs
Paprika, parsley, salt and pepper

Prepare Hollandaise sauce per directions on package. Split English muffins, spread with butter, and toast lightly. Cook bacon in a skillet with about 1 tablespoon butter. Place bacon on each muffin half. Top with an egg; salt and pepper to taste. Spoon warm Hollandaise Sauce over each and sprinkle with paprika and parsley. Serve hot.

Crawfish Omelet

1 pound Crawfish tails
1 stick butter
½ cup chopped green onions
1 clove garlic, crushed
8 eggs
Salt and pepper
½ teaspoon Worcestershire sauce

Fry crawfish tails in butter over low heat until tender. Add onions and garlic. Beat eggs and season with salt, pepper and Worcestershire. Pour over crawfish, stirring gently. When set, turn on a heated platter. Serve immediately.

Kyle LaBlanc www.crawdads.net

Boudin Scramble

Butter
1 link boudin
4 farm-fresh eggs
4 tablespoons milk
Salt and pepper to taste
¼ cup chopped green onions

Warm pan over medium-high heat; add butter to melt. Unlink boudin and heat it through in butter (no need to cook it – that is already done). Scramble eggs with milk and salt and pepper. Once boudin is heated through, pour eggs over boudin. Adjust heat as necessary. Gently mix cooking eggs into boudin, turning as necessary. Once cooked through top with chopped green onions and serve.

Abbeville's Giant Cajun Omelette

5,024 eggs
3 boxes salt
2 boxes black pepper
6½ gallons milk
Tabasco (to taste)
1½ gallons cooking oil

52 pounds butter
50 pounds onions
75 bell peppers
Crawfish tails
2 gallons parsley
4 gallons onion tops

Each year there is one egg added to the "5000 Egg Omelette." In 2009, 5024 eggs are used! Wow!

The Confrerie members gather to crack eggs then pour eggs into 5 gallon buckets. Add salt, pepper, milk and Tabasco. Blend with unique mixing tool (you will have to attend to know what this is) and set aside. Prepare skillet with oil and butter. Add onions and bell pepper; sauté. Add crawfish; sauté. Add egg ingredients to skillet on command. Stir gently and merrily to the beat of Cajun music in the background. Just prior to completion, add parsley and onion tops. Remove skillet from fire. Serve with Poupart's French Bread - C'est Bon!

**Official Ingredients Preparer, Retired Sheriff Ray LeMaire
Giant Omelette Celebration, Abbeville**

GIANT OMELETTE CELEBRATION

First weekend in November · Abbeville

Abbeville's 5000-EGG Giant Omelette Celebration is like no other festival. This family oriented event includes a kids world, arts & crafts show, 3-mile walk through Historic Downtown, antique cars on display, egg cracking contest, and some of Louisiana's best music to get you dancing. Grab your seat early for the procession of chefs, eggs and bread to the Giant 12 foot skillet where fun and folly are the order of day for those preparing the 5000 Egg Giant Omelette.

www.giantomelette.org

Shrimp Salsa Scrambled Eggs over French Bread

6 eggs
½ cup minced salad shrimp
½ cup salsa
Salt and pepper
Hot sauce
Butter
French bread, buttered and toasted

In a bowl, combine eggs, shrimp, and salsa. Season with salt, pepper, and hot sauce to taste; mix well. Slow cook, scrambled egg-style, over medium-low heat with plenty of butter. Spoon on top of French bread. Serve hot.

CAJUN HOT SAUCE FESTIVAL

1st or 2nd Weekend in April • New Iberia

Family oriented festival which includes a variety of food vendors, craft vendors, great musical entertainment & a quality carnival. We also have a hot sauce manufacturer's competition which is judged along with a people's choice winner. On the Sunday of the event we have a Jambalaya Cook-off competition which is co-sponsored by world famous TABASCO Hot Sauce. These cook-off teams have samples of their products (which must include hot sauce) available to the public for tasting.

337.365.7539 • www.sugarena.com

Cajun Breakfast Bake

1 pound ground hot sausage
1 onion, chopped
1 green bell pepper, chopped
1 red bell pepper, chopped
½ tablespoon cayenne pepper
2 tablespoons butter
Garlic powder
2 tubes crescent rolls, divided
2 cups frozen hash browns
2 cups cooked shredded chicken
1½ cups shredded Cheddar cheese
5 eggs
¼ cup milk
Salt and pepper to taste
2 tablespoons Parmesan cheese

Cook sausage with onion, bell peppers, cayenne pepper, butter and garlic powder to taste until sausage is browned; drain and set aside. Layer 1 tube crescent rolls in a baking dish treated with nonstick spray; press over bottom and up sides to form a crust. Pinch and press edges to seal perforations. In a bowl, combine sausage with remaining ingredients. Top with remaining rolls; cover lightly with foil. Bake at 375° for 25 to 30 minutes. The last few minutes of baking, remove foil to brown top.

Tracy and Andy Flores

Tater Bacon Pancakes

⅓ cup finely chopped onion
⅓ cup butter, divided
4 cups cooked mashed potatoes
2 eggs, beaten
½ cup flour
⅓ cup real bacon bits or minced ham
Milk

Cook onion in about half the butter until onion is golden. Remove with a slotted spoon and combine with mashed potatoes, eggs, flour, and bacon bits; add milk to thin to loose batter. Pour or spoon into a hot skillet cooking in butter like a thick pancake.

Cheese, Bacon and Shrimp Grits

4 cups water
1 teaspoon salt
1 cup grits
3 tablespoons butter or margarine
1 cup shredded cheese
⅓ cup real bacon bits
⅓ cup salad shrimp, thawed and well drained
4 tablespoons butter
Hot Sauce

Bring water to a boil. Add salt, and slowly stir in grits. Stir well, frequently, to prevent lumping. Reduce heat and cover; simmer 10 minutes. Stir in cheese, bacon bits, and shrimp. Serve hot with butter and a dash of hot sauce.

Bernice Caulter

Grits and Grillades

2 pounds boneless beef round
    steak, about ¼-inch thick
½ cup all-purpose flour
1 tablespoon salt
1 teaspoon cayenne
1 teaspoon black pepper
¼ cup vegetable oil
2 yellow onions, diced
1 red or green bell pepper, diced
2 ribs celery, diced
3 cloves garlic, chopped
1½ cups whole canned tomatoes, crushed with their juice
1 cup beef broth
¼ cup dry red wine
1 bay leaf
½ teaspoon dried thyme
½ teaspoon dried basil
Prepared grits (5 servings)
¼ cup finely chopped green onions

This classic Creole dish is a brunch staple in households and restaurants around New Orleans. At its simplest, a "grillade" is pounded round steak that has been seared to a deep brown, then braised in a spicy, rich gravy. It can be made with beef or pork, or in the true spirit of Southern decadence, veal. The thick stew is served ladled over hot, toothsome grits and garnished with a sprinkle of green onion.

Trim fat from beef and cut into 2-inch squares. Combine flour, salt, cayenne and black pepper in a small bowl. Dredge meat through seasoned flour mix. With a meat mallet, gently pound beef until flattened; dredge again. In a large, heavy pot, heat oil over medium-high heat. Add meat, several pieces at a time (but not all at once, to avoid crowding), and sear to a dark, crusty brown on both sides. Transfer to a platter and repeat with remaining pieces. Return all meat to the pot. Add onions, bell peppers, celery and garlic. Cook, stirring occasionally, until vegetables are soft and golden, about 10 minutes. Stir in tomatoes and liquid, broth, wine, bay leaf, thyme and basil. Reduce heat to medium-low. Simmer, uncovered, stirring occasionally, scraping the sides and bottom of the pan to remove and reincorporate the food. Cook until meat is very tender, about 1½ hours. If mixture becomes dry, add more broth. Serve over hot grits and garnish with green onion. Makes about 5 servings.

Colleen Rush, Louisiana native and author of "The Mere Mortal's Guide to Fine Dining"

Three-Cheese Crawfish Quiche

½ cup chopped onions
1 tablespoon vegetable oil
1 medium tomato, chopped and drained
2 cups cooked rice
¼ teaspoon salt
¼ teaspoon pepper
1 cup chopped, cooked spinach
2 cups Louisiana crawfish tail meat
½ cup shredded Swiss cheese
½ cup shredded mozzarella cheese
5 eggs, beaten
⅔ cup light cream
1 teaspoon Cajun or Creole seasoning
¼ teaspoon nutmeg
¼ teaspoon cayenne pepper
¼ cup grated Parmesan cheese

Cook onions in oil in large skillet over medium heat. Measure ¼ cup tomatoes and set aside; stir remaining tomatoes into onions in skillet. Add rice, salt and pepper; cook 2 to 3 minutes. Press into a greased 9-inch deep-dish pie plate. Spread spinach over rice mixture, top with crawfish, then with Swiss and mozzarella cheeses. Combine eggs, cream, Cajun or Creole seasoning, nutmeg and cayenne in a small bowl. Pour over cheese layer. Sprinkle with reserved tomato, then with Parmesan cheese. Bake at 350° for 35 to 40 minutes or until firm and golden brown. Serves 6.

Kyle LaBlanc www.crawdads.net

Cajun Tomato Quiche

1 onion, chopped
1 cup diced tomatoes, roasted
½ cup chopped green bell pepper
2 large garlic cloves, minced
1 tablespoon minced jalapeño pepper
1 teaspoon red pepper flakes
3 to 4 tablespoons chopped cilantro
6 eggs
1 cup half and half (or whole milk)
1 teaspoon salt
1 cup (4 ounces) shredded sharp Cheddar cheese
1 deep-dish pie crust, thawed

Combine everything, except pie crust, in a bowl; mix well. (If want to roast your own tomatoes, sprinkle them with a bit of olive oil and broil in the oven until edges are toasted.) Spoon into pie crust. Bake at 400° for 30 minutes. You can increase the ingredients slightly and stretch this to make two regular-size quiches rather than one deep dish.

Bernice Caulter

THE CREOLE TOMATO FESTIVAL, THE CAJUN-ZYDECO FESTIVAL AND THE LOUISIANA SEAFOOD FESTIVAL

June • New Orleans

A New Orleans Vieux to Do celebrates 3 festivals in one weekend, in the New Orleans French Market. The Creole Tomato Festival, The Cajun-Zydeco Festival and the Louisiana Seafood Festival. It is held on Saturday and Sunday usually in June. There is plenty for the whole family to enjoy, lots of great food, music and art. For more information visit, www.LouisianaSeafoodFestival.com

504.286.8735 • www.frenchmarket.org • www.louisianaseafood.com

Cajun No-Shell Quiche

4 to 6 eggs
½ cup water
½ cup buttermilk
½ cup plain nonfat yogurt
2 tablespoons grated fresh Parmesan cheese
½ teaspoon dry mustard
¼ teaspoon hot sauce
1 cup shredded Cheddar cheese
¾ cup chopped lean ham
½ cup chopped green onions
1 can chopped green chilies
⅓ cup minced celery
1 tablespoon hot sauce

Combine ingredients in a bowl; mix well. Pour into a baking dish treated with nonstick spray. Bake at 350° for 40 minutes or until set and browned. Serve hot.

Brandy Peaches

6 large peaches,
    peeled and sliced
1 cup sifted powdered sugar, divided
2 cups whipping cream
⅓ cup peach brandy
1½ teaspoons vanilla extract

Place peaches in a medium bowl; sprinkle with ½ cup powdered sugar until evenly coated. Beat cream with an electric mixer on medium-high speed until peaks just begin to form. Beat in remaining ½ cup powdered sugar, peach brandy and vanilla. Beat just until soft peaks form. Fold into peaches and serve.

Bobbi Lynne's Sweet Potato Mini-Muffins

1 box bread mix,
   (either pumpkin, sweet potato, or spice)
⅔ cup Egg Beaters "All Whites" (5 egg whites)
½ cup cinnamon applesauce
½ tablespoon butter (half a pat), melted
¾ cup pureed Louisiana sweet potatoes
⅓ cup water
½ teaspoon ground cloves
½ teaspoon ground nutmeg

A delicious, quick and healthy favorite that uses Louisiana sweet potatoes to make a great guilt-free snack, side dish, or even dessert.

Preheat oven to 400°. Combine all ingredients in a large mixing bowl and beat until smooth. Let rest for 15 minutes. Spray mini-muffin pans with cooking spray; fill cups ⅔ full. Bake 15 minutes, remove to a cooling rack. Yields 12 servings of 3 mini-muffins, with 150 calories per serving. If all the servings aren't devoured in one sitting, store in the fridge in a large plastic bag, and warm 10 seconds in the microwave before serving.

Bobbi Lynne Shackelford, Lafayette

LECOMPTE PIE FESTIVAL

First Weekend in October • Lecompte

The Lecompte Pie Festival was organized in 2000 under the administration of Former Mayor Rosa Jones. Lecompte was noted for Lea's Restaurant and the pies they send all over the world. Thanks to Former Representative Charlie Dewitt, a bill was passed making Lecompte the Pie Capital of Louisiana. That's how our festival begun. The first weekend in October each year, we celebrate The Lecompte Pie Festival with food and craft booths, entertainment, pageant, parade, rides and games for the children. The first year the festival kicked off with 12,000 plus in attendance.

318.776.5488 • www.asliceoflouisiana.com

Salads, Sauces, Dressings & Rubs

Grandaddy's Hot Potato Salad

2½ teaspoons dry mustard
1 teaspoon water
⅓ teaspoon sugar
⅔ cup vinegar
6 medium potatoes, boiled about 32 minutes and chopped
½ bell pepper, chopped
6 sprigs parsley, chopped
4 cloves garlic, minced
1 large onion, chopped
2 large stalks celery, finely chopped
1 teaspoon red pepper
1 heaping teaspoon salt
1 teaspoon black pepper
1 pint mayonnaise

*From North Louisiana
(Circa 1920's)*

Make a paste from mustard and water; let stand 10 minutes. Add sugar; let stand 5 minutes. Stir in vinegar and combine with remaining ingredients. Mix very well to allow ingredients a chance to exchange their flavors.

Kathleen Robinson from the "Robinson & Stirling Family Recipe Collection"

Exotic Chicken Salad

4 cups cooked, chopped chicken
2 cans sliced water chestnuts
1 cup finely chopped celery
1 pound seedless grapes
1 cup toasted sliced almonds
1 cup mayonnaise
1 teaspoon curry powder
1 tablespoon soy sauce
1 tablespoon lemon juice
Lettuce for serving (optional)
1 (16-ounce) can pineapple chunks

Wonderful for a shower or on hot summer day.

Combine chicken, water chestnuts, celery, grapes, and almonds. Mix mayo, curry, soy sauce and lemon juice. Add seasoned mayo to chicken mixture mixing well. Chill several hours. Serve over lettuce topped with pineapple chunks. Tasty! Serves 10 to 12.

Dale Tully, Homer

Grape Salad

4 packages sweetener
2 pounds seedless black grapes (slice if not small)
8 ounces sour cream
½ to 1 teaspoon almond flavoring
¾ cup chopped pecans

Sprinkle sweetener over grapes. Add sour cream; mix. Add flavoring and pecans, mix. Chill before serving.

Pauline Butler, Bentley

Coke Salad

1 small jar cherries
1 large can crushed pineapple
1 large (2 small) packages Cherry Jell-O
1 cup pecans
1 (4-ounce) package cream cheese, softened (optional)
2 cups (16 ounces) Coca-Cola

Drain cherries and pineapple, reserving juice. Heat juices to boiling. In the meantime, cut cherries in half and set aside. Remove boiling juice from water and stir in Jell-O until dissolved. Add fruit, nuts, cream cheese, and Coke; mix well. Chill before serving. Enjoy!

Note: Marshmallows can be substituted for the cream cheese—kids love this. I've even used green cherries during the holidays.

Cindy D. Ezernack
Zwolle Tamale Fiesta, Zwolle

ZWOLLE TAMALE FIESTA

Second Full Weekend in October • Zwolle

The Zwolle Tamale Fiesta celebrates the rich Spanish and Indian heritage of the people of the town. Held each year at the Zwolle Festival Grounds, it is a fun-filled weekend of reliving the area's heritage with plenty of delicious hot tamales, entertainment, arts and crafts, dancing, parades, and children's activities. The Fiesta is fun for the entire family.

318.645.6141/318.645.2388 • www.zwollela.net

Pretzel Strawberry Salad

Layer 1:

2 cups crushed pretzels
¾ cup melted margarine
1 tablespoon sugar

Mix well. Press into 9x13-inch Pyrex dish. Bake 8 minutes at 350°. Cool.

Layer 2:

1 cup sugar
1 small container cool whip
2 (8-ounce) packages cream cheese, softened

Cream Layer 2 ingredients together thoroughly. Spread over cooled first layer.

Layer 3:

1 large strawberry jello
2 cups boiling water
2 (10-ounce) package frozen strawberries

Dissolve jello in water. Add frozen strawberries and mix well. Chill until thickened. Spread over second layer. Chill. Serve in squares. Serves 20.

Evelyn White, Starks

STRAWBERRY FESTIVAL

April · Ponchatoula

The Strawberry Festival has blossomed into a Louisiana celebration second only to Mardi Gras in its magnitude. We are the second largest free festival in the state. Are are many fun family events including Strawberry Ball, Baking Contest, Talent Show and Pageant. Plus you will enjoy live entertainment, rides, food booths, a parade, and so much more. Join us in Ponchatoula for a Strawberry Good Time!

1.800.917.7045 • www.lastrawberryfestival.com

Crab & Red Tater Salad

1 pound small red-skinned potatoes
¼ teaspoon salt
1 cup crabmeat
3 scallions (white part only), finely chopped
2 tablespoons chopped parsley
¼ teaspoon grated lemon zest
1 tablespoon olive oil
2 teaspoon fresh lemon juice
Salt and pepper to taste

Quarter potatoes, with skins. Boil until they are easily pierced with the tip of a knife (about 15 minutes). Drain and transfer to a mixing bowl. Add crabmeat, scallions, parsley and lemon zest. Toss with a fork to combine. Mix in oil and lemon juice. Season to taste.

Tangy Coleslaw

1 head cabbage, chopped
1½ cups mayonnaise
3 tablespoons Dijon mustard
2 teaspoons lemon juice
3 tablespoons white vinegar
1 teaspoon Creole seasoning

Chop cabbage into thin slices and cut to bite size pieces. Add remaining ingredients, except Creole seasoning, mix well. Cover and chill until ready to serve. Sprinkle Creole seasoning over top before serving.

Crawdad Slaw

½ head cabbage,
    shredded
½ cup finely chopped carrots
1 cup minced cooked crawfish meat, cooled
½ cup mayonnaise
Black pepper to taste
Dash vinegar
Dash sugar

Shred cabbage and combine with all ingredients. Cover and chill least 30 minutes before serving.

Jeanne's Cabbage Slaw

1 large head cabbage
3 to 5 green onions, finely chopped
1 cup mayonnaise
2 cans lump crabmeat, drained
Juice of ½ lemon

Shred cabbage and mix with remaining ingredients in a large bowl. Refrigerate and serve cold.

Christmas Celebration & Gumbo Cookoff, Morganza

Spicy Tomato Relish

1 cup coarsely chopped tomato
2 tablespoons ketchup
¼ cup chopped celery
1 small green pepper, chopped
1 small onion, chopped
1 teaspoon coarsely chopped parsley
⅛ teaspoon hot pepper sauce
Large dash garlic salt
1 tablespoon hot sauce
Large dash oregano

Combine all ingredients. Cover and chill. Blend for a finer relish.

Raisin Cranberry Relish

2¼ cups golden raisins
½ cup finely chopped pecans
2 cups orange juice
1 cup water
½ cup sugar
⅓ cup lemon juice
3 cups frozen cranberries
1 tablespoon orange zest

Combine ingredients in a saucepan and simmer until reduced by half. Remove from heat and cool. Cover; chill before serving.

Hot Tomato Relish

½ cup plain salt (not iodized)
1 gallon chopped or quartered green tomatoes
½ gallon chopped or quartered white onions
1 quart chopped green bell peppers
3 cups sugar
½ cup chopped hot peppers
1 quart white vinegar
2 tablespoons black pepper

Pour salt over chopped tomatoes; set aside (this will make tomatoes crisp and will make some juice). Mix all ingredients well in large pan and simmer until tender and bell pepper is no longer a bright green. The longer cooked, the softer the tomatoes. Cool before serving.

Bobbie McInnis

Creamy Creole Salad Dressing

1 cup plain yogurt
3 tablespoon Creole mustard
1 tablespoon white vinegar
Dash oil

Mix yogurt and mustard. Add vinegar. Stir well. Add oil to thin as needed. Chill and serve.

Remoulade Dressing

Dressing:

1 cup olive oil

⅓ cup wine vinegar

½ cup finely chopped onion

1 cup chopped celery

3 tablespoons creole mustard

3 tablespoons horseradish

2 tablespoons paprika

1 teaspoon Tabasco

1 teaspoon salt

1 teaspoon black pepper

½ teaspoon cayenne pepper

1 cup mayonnaise

2 tablespoons chopped parsley

Combine all ingredients in food processor, (or bowl) pulse (or mix) briefly to blend. Serve cold with seafood (see below). Yields ⅔ quart.

Seafood:

1 pound Louisiana crawfish

1 pound Louisiana jumbo lump crabmeat

2 pounds Louisiana peeled and deveined shrimp (40/50) cooked

Combine Remoulade Sauce with Louisiana Seafood. Chill and serve.

Chef Tommy Cvitanovich & Seafood Promotion and Marketing Board

Citrus Pecan Vinaigrette

½ shallot, chopped
3 tablespoons Dijon mustard
⅓ cup crushed pecans
⅓ cup orange juice
⅓ cup lemon juice
⅓ cup lime juice
1½ teaspoons salt
¼ teaspoon pepper
1 cup olive oil

Place shallots, mustard, pecans, juices, salt and pepper in a food processor. Process thoroughly, so that shallot is finely minced in the liquid. With machine running, slowly drizzle olive oil into mixture until emulsified.

Cucumber Dressing

1 cup mayonnaise
1 cup buttermilk
2 medium cucumber, peeled, seeded, and pureed
2 tablespoons finely chopped shallots
2 teaspoons chopped parsley
2 teaspoons celery powder
1 garlic clove, minced
¼ teaspoon onion powder
¼ teaspoon paprika
⅛ teaspoon cayenne pepper
Salt and pepper to taste

Combine all ingredients, mixing well. Place in container with lid and refrigerate at least 2 hours before using.

Honey Dressing

⅔ cup sugar
5 tablespoons white vinegar
1½ tablespoons lemon juice
¾ cup canola oil
½ cup honey
2 teaspoons paprika
1 teaspoon celery seed
1 teaspoon minced onion
Black pepper to taste

Combine sugar, vinegar, and lemon juice in a saucepan over medium-high heat. Bring to a boil and continue to boil 1 minute. Remove from heat and pour into electric blender. Add everything except canola oil and blend. Slowly add canola oil, continuing to blend slowly. When well blended, transfer to a cruet or other lidded container. Shake before serving.

Louisiana Italian Dressing

1 cup olive oil
¼ cup cider vinegar
1 tablespoon hot sauce
1 teaspoon garlic powder
1 teaspoon onion powder
2 teaspoons Italian seasoning
1 teaspoon paprika
2 teaspoons grated Parmesan cheese

Combine all in a bowl and mix well. Keep refrigerated.

Creole Oil & Vinegar Dressing

⅓ cup vegetable oil
3 tablespoons olive oil
3 tablespoons cider vinegar
1 teaspoon sugar
1 teaspoon salt
Juice of 1 lemon
Freshly-ground black pepper

Place all ingredients in a container with a lid and shake well to combine. Keep refrigerated. Remember to shake each time before using.

Honey Mustard Vinaigrette

1 cup apple cider vinegar
⅓ cup honey
2 tablespoons Dijon mustard
1 tablespoon oil
1 tablespoon salted sunflower seeds

Combine all ingredients in a bowl and mix. Cover and chill overnight if possible.

Cajun Yogurt Salad Dressing

1 cup plain yogurt
1 tablespoon lemon juice
1 to 2 tablespoons milk
1 teaspoon dried parsley
1 teaspoon dried dillweed
½ teaspoon garlic powder
½ teaspoon black pepper

Combine all ingredients in a bowl. Cover and chill for at least 30 minutes before serving.

Creole Blue Cheese Dressing

4 ounce crumbled blue cheese
1 cup sour cream
1 teaspoon lemon juice
1 teaspoon sugar
1 teaspoon finely-minced onion
Dash garlic powder
Dash hot sauce
½ teaspoon salt

Mix all ingredients and chill in refrigerator.

Mustard Dressing

2 tablespoons apple juice
1 tablespoon lemon juice
5 tablespoon Creole mustard
Dash hot sauce

Mix all ingredients in one jar. The taste is enhanced with age.
Keep refrigerated.

Creole Tarter Sauce

¼ cup finely chopped celery
¼ cup finely chopped green onions
¼ cup finely chopped parsley
3 tablespoons mayonnaise
3 tablespoons tomato paste
3 tablespoons Dijon-style mustard
1 tablespoon olive oil
1 tablespoon white wine vinegar
¾ teaspoon hot sauce
½ teaspoon paprika

In small bowl, combine all ingredients until well blended.

Crab Cake Tarter Sauce

1 cup mayonnaise
½ cup sour cream
¼ cup milk
⅓ cup sweet relish
1½ tablespoons hot sauce
½ tablespoon chili powder
½ tablespoon minced onion
Dash each parsley, white vinegar and garlic powder
Black pepper to taste

Combine all ingredients in a bowl, chill and serve

A quick sauce for crab cakes, crawdad cakes and just about any seafood.

White Remoulade Sauce

3 cups mayonnaise
1 cup Creole mustard
1 tablespoon lemon juice
1 tablespoon Worcestershire sauce
1 tablespoon Tabasco
2 ounces capers with juice
4 ounces onion, finely diced

Mix all ingredients and puree in a blender. Makes a little more than a quart.

Chef Ross Headlee, Louisiana Culinary Institute

Mayo Sauce

1 cup mayonnaise
1 tablespoon dill pickle, minced
1 teaspoon Worcestershire
2 teaspoons brown mustard
1 small onion, minced
1 clove garlic, minced
1 small green bell pepper, minced
1 tablespoon minced parsley

Combine everything in a bowl and mix well. Cover and chill before serving.

Tomato Basil Cream Sauce

1 pint heavy cream
3 ounces tomato paste
½ cup chopped fresh basil
1 cup chopped fresh tomato

I use this for everything from grilled chicken to a seafood sauce. It's also great with pork chops.

Heat cream until ⅓ reduced. Add tomato paste, basil and tomato. Cook over low heat about 10 minutes.

Stephen Nash, Baton Rouge

Steve's Bernaise Sauce

2 sticks unsalted butter
2 tablespoons finely chopped shallots
2 tablespoons tarragon vinegar
1 teaspoon freshly ground black pepper
1 teaspoon dried tarragon
2 egg yolks
1 tablespoon cold water
Salt to taste

I make this sauce for just about anything. It's great with steaks and pork. It may sound a bit difficult, but once you have done it, it is soooo easy.

Melt butter slowly in a small saucepan. Heat shallots, vinegar, pepper and tarragon in another small saucepan and cook until liquid evaporates. Remove from heat. Allow to cool slightly then add egg yolks and water. Return saucepan to stove and stir yolk mixture over very low heat. Do not overheat or eggs will curdle. Remove from heat and place on a cold surface. Stir in melted butter slowly.

Steve Arlen, GO SAINTS

DELCAMBRE SHRIMP FESTIVAL

Third Full Weekend in August • Delcambre

The town of Delcambre, Louisiana, located about 20 miles southwest of Lafayette, is home to one of the area's most productive shrimp fleets. The town devotes an entire weekend to honor this economic lifeblood. Events include a shrimp cook-off, queens pageants, fais-do-do's, food booths, carnival rides, and the blessing of the shrimp boat fleet. There's plenty of fun for kids of all ages and lots to see, hear, and EAT!

337.685.2653 • www.shrimpfestival.net

Bourbon Mustard Mop

¾ cup bourbon
¾ cup mustard
¾ cup cider vinegar
½ cup water
2 tablespoons black pepper
2 tablespoons hot sauce

I use this as a mop and a marinade for cooking on the grill.

Combine all in a bowl and mop as you grill. Great with meats of all type.

Steve Arlen, GO SAINTS

Butter Barbecue Sauce

1½ sticks butter, melted
⅓ cup water
2 medium onions, minced
½ tablespoon cayenne pepper
1 cup ketchup
½ cup cider vinegar
¼ cup fresh orange juice
¼ cup maple syrup
2 tablespoons Worcestershire sauce
Salt and pepper

Combine all ingredients in a saucepan and simmer 30 minutes on low.

Butter Cream Sauce

2 sticks butter
1½ cups sour cream
½ tablespoon cayenne pepper
¼ teaspoon seasoned or onion salt
1 tablespoon chopped chives
Pepper to taste

Melt butter in a small saucepan over low heat. Stir in sour cream, cayenne, seasoned salt and chives. Warm, but do not boil. Serve as dipping sauce.

BBQ Shrimp Butter

1 pound butter, divided
3 ounces shallots, finely diced
3 ounces garlic, finely diced
1 ounce freshly squeezed lemon juice
1 ounce veal jus, cold (veal stock)
2 tablespoons chopped fresh rosemary
1½ teaspoons chopped fresh thyme
Dash cayenne pepper
1½ teaspoons freshly ground black pepper
1 teaspoon Lea & Perrins Worcestershire sauce
1½ teaspoons salt
1 tablespoon paprika

Place chopped shallots in a plastic container with 1 ounce butter. Cover with plastic wrap and microwave 2½ minutes. Cool. Repeat with chopped garlic. Place remaining butter in mixer with paddle and whip until light. Add all ingredients and mix until incorporated. Roll in 1-pound logs in parchment paper and refrigerate or freeze.

Chef G. W. Fins, Seafood Promotion and Marketing Board

Lemon Onion Seafood Marinade

2 lemons, juiced
2 tablespoons soy sauce
½ cup white wine
½ cup minced onion
Dash pepper
Dash garlic powder

Combine all ingredients in a glass bowl and spoon over fish before cooking.

Ben's Tiger Tailgate Marinade

3 tablespoons soy sauce
3 tablespoons orange juice
2 tablespoons olive oil
1 cup ketchup
1 tablespoon minced parsley leaves
1 garlic clove, minced
1 tablespoon lemon juice
½ tablespoon oregano
1 tablespoon pepper

We double and triple this recipe as needed. It's great as a marinade for just about any meat or brushed on burgers on the grill.

This is the best swordfish marinade I have ever made. Whisk everything together, marinate the swordfish in it for an hour, and grill.

Ben & Linda Campbell, LSU Football Fans

Steve's Saints BBQ Rib Rub

⅓ cup ground black pepper
¼ cup paprika
2 tablespoon sugar
1 tablespoon salt
1 tablespoon chili powder
1½ teaspoons garlic powder
1½ teaspoons onion powder

This is perfect for just about anything I have rubbed it on. I even sprinkle over cooked hot dogs and sausages while on a bun.

Mix well and rub into meat before cooking.

Steve Arlen, GO SAINTS

THE SMOKIN' BLUES & BBQ CHALLENGE

Last Weekend in March • Hammond

The Hammond Blues & BBQ Challenge is the largest BBQ Contest in the State of Louisiana and is the State Championship for The Kansas City BBQ Society. Over 120 BBQ teams competing in three different divisions vie for The Grand Championship each year. We are in our 6th year and all proceeds go towards three beneficiaries that help children and families in our community. This year we will benefit Special Olympics Louisiana, TARC & Tangi Food Pantry. Live music nightly, BBQ vendors and drink booths round out our event. Join us for Smokin' Good Time.

985.419.9863 • hammondbluesandbbq.com

Soups, Stews & Gumbo

North Louisiana Broccoli 'n Swiss Soup

1 cup chopped ham
1 cup water
½ cup chopped celery
1 small green bell pepper, chopped
1 can whole kernel corn
1 (10-ounce) package frozen chopped broccoli
2 cups milk
1 tablespoon Cajun seasoning
3 tablespoons flour
1 teaspoon salt
Dash pepper
2 cups cubed Swiss cheese

This recipe is one I made when I camped. It's a combination of Texas and Arkansas with a little bit of Southern Cajun.

Boil ham in water 10 minutes; add remaining ingredients except cheese. Cook until veggies are tender. Slowly add in cheese and cook on low until cheese melts. Add a bit of water or milk to thin to desired thickness.

The Barner Family, North Louisiana

Taco Soup

1½ pounds turkey,
 chicken or ground beef
1 onion, chopped
1 can whole kernel corn (with juice)
1 can pinto beans (with juice)
1 can black beans (with juice)
1 can red beans (with juice)
1 can rotel tomatoes (with juice)
2 cans stewed tomatoes (with juice)
1½ cups water
1 package taco seasoning mix
1 package original-style ranch dressing

Brown meat; drain. Add onion and sauté. Add remaining ingredients. Simmer 1 hour.

Kathleen Robinson from the "Robinson & Stirling Family Recipe Collection"

Beef and Pasta Soup

2 tablespoons olive oil
1 pound ground beef
2 medium green bell peppers, chopped
1 large onion, chopped
Salt and pepper to taste
6 cloves garlic, minced
2 cans tomato paste
3 tomatoes, chopped
2 carrots, finely chopped
5 cups water
1 cup milk
1 teaspoon thyme
1 teaspoon basil
2 teaspoons oregano
1 tablespoon dried parsley leaves
2 cups uncooked elbow pasta (or similar)
Salt and pepper to taste
Freshly grated Parmesan cheese to taste

Brown ground beef in olive oil; drain. Add bell peppers and onions with a bit more oil. Combine all ingredients, except salt, pepper, and Parmesan cheese, in a large stock pot; cover and simmer over medium-low heat for about 1 hour. Add salt and pepper to taste. Serve sprinkled with Parmesan Cheese and a side of toasted French Bread.

Hot Crab Soup

1½ cups crabmeat
1 can cream of mushroom soup
1 can cream of celery soup
1½ soup cans milk
2 tablespoons hot sauce
1 stick butter or margarine
½ tablespoon Creole seasoning
Parsley
Bacon bits

Combine all ingredients, except parsley and bacon bits, in a large saucepan. Cook over low heat until heated through. Do not cook on high. Cook 15 to 20 minutes or until hot. Serve hot topped with parsley flakes and bacon bits.

Charlie Tucker

Crab Soup

½ cup margarine
½ cup chopped shallots
2 cans cream of mushroom soup
2 empty soup cans of milk
1 pound Louisiana white crab meat
1 teaspoon liquid crab boil
1 pint half and half
Salt and pepper

In a 6 quart pot, sauté shallots in margarine until wilted. Add all other ingredients. Bring to a boil. Lower fire and simmer 20 minutes. Stir often and gently.

Chef Darla Kiffe & Seafood Promotion and Marketing Board

Memorial Day Fish Soup

1 pound red snapper,
  boned and cleaned
½ pound shrimp meat, diced
1 onion, finely chopped
1 can diced tomatoes
1 can tomato soup
1 tablespoon hot sauce
½ stick butter
1 bay leaf
Salt and pepper to taste
4 cups water
Dash lemon juice

Combine all the ingredients in a pot and cook over medium heat 30 minutes or until onions are tender. Serve hot.

PLAQUEMINES PARISH HERITAGE AND SEAFOOD FESTIVAL
Memorial Day Weekend ◆ Belle Chasse

Plaquemines Parish Heritage and Seafood Festival is an annual celebration of the rich and vibrant heritage of the people of Plaquemines Parish Louisiana. Visitors to this "Southern Louisiana" treat will enjoy great local seafood and other unique local food specialties fixed as only bayou folks can, along with continuous live music from traditional Cajun instruments for two-stepppin' to local popular rockin' cover bands, crafts from local artisans, carnival rides, helicopter rides over some of the most historical battlefields in the Nation as well as the Mississippi River, the greatest commerce highway in the nation, and fun for the entire family.

504.394.6328 ◆ www.plaqueminesparishfestival.com

Shrimp and Corn Soup

2 ounces (4 tablespoons) butter
2 ounces (scant ½ cup) flour
½ cup finely diced onions
¼ cup each finely diced bell pepper and finely diced celery
1 cup corn (frozen or cut fresh from the cob)
1 tablespoon minced garlic
2 ounces white wine
½ teaspoon each thyme, basil and parsley
2 teaspoons salt
¼ teaspoons each white pepper and cayenne pepper
1 ounce (2 tablespoons) fresh lemon juice
1½ pints (3 cups) whole milk (more or less)
8 ounces (50 to 60 count) shrimp, peeled and deveined
Liason to finish (1 egg yolk to 2 to 3 ounces heavy whipping cream)
Salt, pepper and cayenne to taste

In a 2-quart saucepan over high heat, melt butter and add flour to make a white roux. Cook briefly to incorporate flour thoroughly with butter and then add onions, bell pepper, celery and corn. Sweat the mixture, stirring occasionally, until vegetables are translucent. Add garlic and continue cooking, stirring often, over high heat for 1 minute. Deglaze the mixture with white wine. Add thyme, basil, parsley, salt and peppers. Continue cooking and stirring occasionally for 1 to 2 minutes and then slowly incorporate the milk, making a smooth creamy liquid (more or less milk may be required to achieve a cream-soup liquid consistency). Bring soup to a simmer, lower heat, and continue simmering 20 to 30 minutes or until vegetables are thoroughly cooked. Add shrimp and continue to simmer 10 minutes longer or until pink. Remove from heat and incorporate the liason. Adjust seasonings and serve hot garnished with a cooked shrimp and finely chopped parsley in each bowl.

Chef Ross Headlee, Louisiana Culinary Institute

Butternut Squash & Shrimp Soup

2 pounds headless shrimp in shells
Seasonings (shrimp boil or salt, pepper, cayenne, tabasco and lemon juice)
1 medium-large onion, small dice
2 ribs celery, small dice
1 stick margarine
1 heaping tablespoon minced garlic
1 (2½-pound) butternut squash (peeled, seeded and cubed)
1½ teaspoons salt
½ teaspoon pepper
2 bay leaves
5 tablespoons flour
6 cups shrimp or chicken stock
2½ to 3 cups half & half

In large pot, season water with shrimp boil seasonings. Bring to a rapid boil and add shrimp. Cover and bring back to a boil (about 5 to 6 minutes). Boil 1 minute more. Turn off heat and let shrimp soak 30 minutes. With a slotted spoon, remove shrimp to another bowl and let cool. Pour shrimp stock through a sieve into another large bowl and reserve the stock. Peel shrimp, when cooled. Set aside. Sauté onion and celery in margarine until soft. Add garlic and squash; cook over medium heat 20 to 25 minutes. Add seasonings; stir. Slowly dust with flour, 1 tablespoon at a time, carefully stirring to blend in smoothly. Slowly add 4 cups stock, stirring until blended. Simmer on low 15 minutes. Add half the peeled shrimp and simmer a few minutes more. Turn off heat and let soup mixture cool. Dice the other half of shrimp and set aside. In a blender, puree cooled soup mixture. Place pureed mixture in a large pot and add remaining 2 cups stock, reserved diced shrimp and enough half & half to desired consistency. Warm over low heat and serve. DO NOT bring mixture to a boil or the cream will separate!

Jill Carney, Baton Rouge

Baked Potato Soup

2 tablespoons ham base
2 quarts chicken broth
1½ cups diced onions
1½ sticks margarine, divided
2 pounds potatoes, small dice
1½ teaspoons black pepper
3 cups heavy cream
½ cup shredded Cheddar cheese

Combine ham base with chicken broth; stir until smooth. In a large stockpot, sauté onions in 6 tablespoons margarine until clear. Add potatoes and black pepper. Add broth and bring to a boil and cook until potatoes are very tender. In a separate pan, melt remaining 6 tablespoons margarine; add flour to make a roux. Cook over medium-low heat, stirring constantly, until light golden brown. When soup is boiling, add roux beating well with a wire whisk until well combined. Return to a boil. Add cream; mix well. Add Cheddar cheese; mix well. To serve, top with more cheese, chopped green onions, and/or crumbled bacon, if desired.

Allen Parish, Oberlin

Shrimp Bisque

¼ cup butter
1 large onion, chopped
½ cup chopped celery
2 cloves garlic, minced
2 tablespoons flour
2 tablespoons tomato paste
3 cups milk
2 cups clam or fish broth
1 bay leaf
½ teaspoon dried basil leaves
½ teaspoon hot sauce
¼ teaspoon salt
1 pound shrimp, peeled and deveined
¼ cup sliced green onions

Melt butter in a large pot. Add onion, celery and garlic; cook until tender. Stir in flour and tomato paste; cook 1 minute. Remove from heat. Gradually stir in milk and broth; add bay leaf, basil, hot sauce and salt. Bring to a boil. Reduce heat; simmer 10 minutes. Add shrimp and green onions; simmer 5 minutes longer or until shrimp turn pink. Remove bay leaf before serving.

SEAFOOD FESTIVAL

4th of July Weekend • Mandeville

The oldest festival held in St. Tammany Parish, attendance for the Seafood Festival is estimated at over ten thousand people per day. Our association is a non-profit corporation, with a 100% volunteer membership, including the officers who contribute countless hours without compensation. The festival association has donated over $1,000,000.00 to various Mandeville area charities and causes. The festival features 20 food booths serving seafood dishes as well as alternative dishes, arts & craft booths, a children's entertainment area, and live musical entertainment throughout the three day event. The annual fireworks show is choreographed to music and celebrates the 4th of July.

985.624.9762 • www.seafoodfest.com

Crawfish Corn Chowder

3 slices bacon, cut in small pieces
2 tablespoons butter
1 medium onion, chopped
3 to 4 tablespoons flour
2 cups shrimp or chicken stock
1 cup diced raw potatoes
1 bay leaf (optional)
Salt and pepper
Tabasco
1 (16-ounce) can corn
2 cups half & half, warmed
1 pound peeled crawfish tails or shrimp
1 teaspoon lemon juice
¼ bunch parsley
¼ cup finely chopped green onions

Brown bacon lightly for about 5 minutes. Add butter and stir in onions. Cook 2 to 3 minutes, stirring frequently. Add flour, stirring until smoothly blended. Add shrimp stock slowly, constantly stirring until smooth. Add potatoes and simmer until potatoes are tender. Add bay leaf, salt, pepper and tabasco to taste. Add corn and half & half; stir well. Carefully fold in crawfish tails; bring to a boil, then reduce heat to low and simmer 8 to 10 minutes. Correct seasoning; stir in lemon juice. Sprinkle parsley and chives over top before serving.

Jill Carney, Baton Rouge

Crawfish Corn & Potato Chowder

½ cup chopped onion
½ cup chopped celery
1 tablespoon butter
2 cups half & half or milk
12 to 16 ounces crawfish tails
1 large potato (diced, cooked, and drained)
1 (15-ounce) can whole kernel corn (drained)
1 (15-ounce) can cream-style corn
½ teaspoon salt
1 teaspoon Tony Chachere's Creole Seasoning
½ cup chopped green onion (optional)

In a large saucepan, cook onion and celery in butter until tender. Add milk, crawfish, potatoes and corn. Cover and simmer 10 minutes (do not boil), stirring frequently. Season with salt and creole seasoning; stir in green onions. Serve immediately.

Kyle LaBlanc www.crawdads.net

Sausage Tater & Corn Chowder

½ pound smoked sausage
1 onion, chopped
2 tablespoons butter
2 medium potatoes, chopped
2 cups water
1 teaspoon salt
½ teaspoon pepper
2 cans sweet corn
½ pound cooked ham, chopped
1 (13-ounce) can evaporated milk
¼ cup flour
½ cup water

Fry sausage and onion in butter until onions are soft and sausage is browned. Combine with remaining ingredients in a large saucepan or pot. Include some of the drippings from the skillet. Cover and cook on low, stirring, until thickened. Add water or flour as needed.

Louisiana Oyster Chowder

8 to 10 Louisiana oysters
Butter
1 onion, finely chopped
1 cup finely chopped celery
1 red bell pepper, finely chopped
1 can green chilies
1 potato, diced
1½ tablespoons flour
1½ quarts milk
1½ cups cream
½ cup real bacon bits
Salt and pepper to taste
1 tablespoon hot sauce

Rinse and drain oysters. Cook oysters in butter about 5 minutes, chopping oysters as you cook. In a saucepan, cook all vegetables in butter. When soft, add flour and mix well. Slowly add milk, whipping all the time. Add cream and let cook 30 minutes. Add oysters; cook about 2 minutes more. Add milk, if needed. Stir in bacon bits and hot sauce then season to taste with salt and pepper just before serving.

OYSTER FESTIVAL

3rd Weekend in March • Amite

Held every third weekend of March the Amite Oyster Festival has held the distinction of being the first festival of the season each year in Tangipahoa Parish since 1976. The oyster industry, which came to Amite in 1949 and has continued to grow each year, is honored with a month long celebration culminating in this festival. Churches, service organizations, school groups and other clubs benefit from this festival, The families that began the oyster industry are still actively involved and are touched and proud to be honored by the wonderful people of Amite. Come to the Amite Oyster Festival to have a shuckin' good time.

985.748.7156 • www.amiteoysterfestival.org

On the Bayou Cajun Chili

2 tablespoons vegetable oil
1 pound beef stew meat
1 pound ground andoullie sausage
1 medium onion, chopped
1 small green bell pepper, chopped
2 cloves garlic, minced
3 tablespoons chili powder
1 teaspoon paprika
½ teaspoon celery seed
½ teaspoon salt
2 cans chili beans
4 cups water
2 tablespoon hot sauce
1 can chopped tomatoes
1 can chopped green chilies

Heat oil in a large pot or Dutch oven. Add stew meat and sausage; cook over medium-high heat until browned. Add remaining ingredients and cover. Simmer about 1 hour, stirring as needed. Add additional water, beans, hot sauce and seasonings to taste.

THE GREAT CHILI CHALLENGE

1st Saturday in November • New Iberia

The Great Chili Challenge is a fun event for the entire family. There are many different chilis to taste and vote on, live music, art and crafts and many fun things for the kids to do. Come and enjoy good food and lots of fun!

337.364.2273

Cajun Chili

2 cans pinto beans
2 cans chili beans
1 pound chopped andoullie sausage, browned
2 pounds ground beef, browned
2 cans beef stock
4 cans water
2 onions, chopped
2 green bell peppers, chopped
½ to 1 cup minced celery
1 teaspoon garlic salt
1 teaspoon onion salt
½ teaspoon thyme
½ teaspoon Marjoram
2 cans stewed tomatoes
1 pack chili seasoning mix
Hot sauce to taste

Combine all ingredients in a large pot and simmer 3 hours or longer.

LYDIA CAJUN FOOD FEST

2nd Weekend in September • Lydia

The Cajun Food Fest is a two-day event beginning Friday from 5pm to Midnight and continuing Saturday from 10am to 9pm. You'll enjoy a fais do do with 3 bands plus food booths, rides for kids, arts & crafts booths, a peoples-choice cook-off, survival walk and poker run. All money raised helps cancer patients in 4 parishes.

337.230.6730 or 337.519.9593

Bacon Shrimp Bayou Chili

1 pound bacon, cooked and crumbled
4 tablespoons reserved bacon drippings
1 onion, chopped
1 pound ground beef, browned
2 tablespoons Cajun or Creole Seasoning
1 tablespoon red pepper flakes
1 tablespoon chili powder
½ tablespoon Italian seasoning
1 teaspoon cumin powder
2 garlic cloves, minced
2 cans tomato soup
1 can onion soup
2 cans chili beans
2 to 3 cups medium shrimp, cooked and shelled (or salad shrimp)

Combine all ingredients, except shrimp, in a pot. Cook over medium-low heat at least an hour. About 10 minutes before serving, stir in shrimp. Serve hot.

Granddaddy's Oyster Bacon Stew

2 cups water
3 dozen small to medium Louisiana oysters
1 stick butter
1 cup freshly chopped celery
1 teaspoon Cajun seasoning
½ cup freshly chopped green onions
½ cup cooked and crumbled bacon
2 cups heavy cream

This is my grandfather's recipe for oyster stew. We have used shrimp in it as well. Enjoy!

Cook all ingredients in a large pot and simmer over medium heat until edges of oysters begin to curl. Serve hot.

Angie Pentier

Beef Stew Louisiana-Style

2 pounds beef chuck, cubed
2 tablespoons vegetable oil
2 tablespoons flour
2 onions, sliced
1 can tomatoes, undrained
2 carrots, thinly sliced
1 large potato, pared and sliced
2 teaspoons salt
1 teaspoon dried thyme leaves
2 tablespoons hot sauce
1 tablespoon minced garlic
1 bay leaf

In large pot or Dutch oven, brown meat in oil. Sprinkle with flour; mix well. Add onions; cook 5 minutes. Add tomatoes, carrots, potato, salt, thyme, hot sauce, garlic and bay leaf. Add water just to cover. Cover pot and simmer over medium-low heat 1½ hours or until meat and vegetables are tender; stir occasionally. Remove bay leaf before serving. Serve over hot cooked rice with a slice of French bread, if desired.

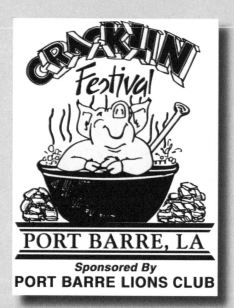

PORT BARRE LIONS CLUB CRACKLIN FESTIVAL

2nd full weekend in November • Port Barre

Our festival is held Thursday thru Sunday in November, featuring a fair, arts and craft booths, food booths, and live music all weekend. You'll enjoy a parade on Saturday and Queens pageant the weekend before. Money raised is donated to Lions Eye Foundation in New Orleans, LA, Lions Crippled Children Camp in Leesville, LA, and various other charities. Thursday night til 10 pm, Friday & Saturday til 12 midnight and Sunday til 6 pm.

337.585.6673 • www.portbarrecracklinfestival.com

Beef Stew

Oil
2½ pounds stew meat
2 cups water
⅓ cup steak sauce
1 tablespoon hot sauce
2 cups diced celery
4 to 6 carrots, diced
4 medium potatoes, diced
2 large onions, diced
2 cans stewed tomatoes
1 can chopped mushrooms
1 can whole kernel corn
½ tablespoon salt
½ tablespoon black pepper
Garlic powder to taste
½ tablespoon basil
½ teaspoon thyme
2 tablespoons sugar
2 teaspoons Worcestershire sauce

Heat oil in stockpot. Brown stew meat. Add remaining ingredients in a stock pot and bring to a simmer. Add more water as needed. Stir in stew meat, cover and simmer about 2 hours. Add water to thin, flour to thicken.

Alligator Stew

½ cup vegetable oil
1 quart cubed alligator meat
½ cup chopped onion
½ cup chopped bell pepper
½ cup chopped celery

2 tablespoons minced parsley
1 (10-ounce) can tomatoes with green chilies
Salt and pepper
1 cup cooked rice

Put vegetable oil and alligator meat in a heavy 4-quart cooking pot. Add chopped vegetables, parsley and tomatoes. Season with salt and pepper. Cover pot and cook over medium heat 1 hour. Serve over hot cooked rice. Preparation time: 1 hour, 15 minutes.

Chef Noah Ciaccio & Seafood Promotion and Marketing Board

Gator Bait Stew

3 cans chicken stock
4 cans water
2 pounds alligator meat, small cubed and browned
1 bay leaf
1 can whole kernel corn
1 tablespoon Worcestershire sauce
1 tablespoon hot pepper sauce

Salt and pepper to taste
2 cans diced tomatoes chilies
1 cup rice
1 or 2 green bell peppers, diced
1 diced onion
1 cup diced carrots
1 cup diced okra
1 cup diced celery

Combine all ingredients in a pot and simmer 1½ hours. Add additional water or cook down stock for desired thickness and add additional seasonings as desired. Remove bay leaf before serving.

Chicken, Duck and Andouille Sausage Gumbo

2 cups sliced okra (¼-inch slices)
1¼ cups oil, divided
1 cup plain flour
2 cups diced onions
2 cups diced celery
1 pound sliced Andouille sausage (¼-inch slices)
12 cups water
1 frying chicken with liver and gizzard, cut-up
1 teal duck or mallard breast, optional (additional chicken may be substituted)
2 tablespoons salt
½ teaspoon black pepper
1 cup chopped green onions
½ cup chopped parsley
2 cups cubed fresh tomato

In a large frying pan, lightly fry okra in ¼ cup oil about 4 to 5 minutes. (Make sure okra is only one layer thick and spread over bottom of frying pan. Frying will cut the slime in the okra.) Set aside. In an 8-quart pot, make a roux with flour and remaining 1 cup oil. When the roux is slightly darker than a grocery bag, immediately stir in onions. Cover, reduce heat and simmer 10 minutes. Add celery, andouille, water, chicken, duck, salt and black pepper. Cover, bring to boil, reduce heat and simmer 1 hour. Skim oil from gumbo. Debone chicken and duck and set aside. To gumbo, add green onions, parsley, tomatoes and okra. Return to a boil; add chicken and duck and cook until chicken is done. Serve over cooked rice.

Note: If a less heavy gumbo is desired, use less roux or none at all, but do not use less of the other ingredients. If fillet is desired, add to individual servings (do not add to pot as this may cause gumbo to spoil).

Kathleen Robinson from the "Robinson & Stirling Family Recipe Collection"

Seafood Gumbo Filé

½ cup cooking oil
¾ cup all-purpose flour
3 quarts water (about)
6 green onions, chopped
1 clove garlic
1 pound smoked sausage, sliced
Salt and pepper, to taste
3 cups peeled and deveined shrimp
½ cup crabmeat
¾ pint oysters
Filé powder

Brown flour in oil until dark brown (use heavy pot, preferably cast iron). Carefully add water. Let this come to a boil; add onions, garlic, sausage, salt and pepper to taste. Allow this to cook slowly 1½ hours. Add shrimp and continue cooking 1 hour. Add crabmeat and oysters; cook about 10 minutes longer. Add more water as necessary to make the consistency you want. Remove from heat. Remove any excess grease. Add file´ to taste (about 1 to 2 tablespoons). Allow to rest for an hour or so before serving.

Elaine Boatwright, Bridge City Gumbo Festival

GUMBO FESTIVAL

Second Weekend in October • Bridge City

In 1973, Bridge City was proclaimed "The Gumbo Capital of the World" which began the annual celebration of the Gumbo Festival. It has grown into one of the most popular festivals of Louisiana attracting festival-goers and visitors from around the world. In addition to the very best seafood and chicken gumbo in the world, ` visitors will experience live entertainment, carnival rides, games, arts and crafts, and a Gumbo Cooking Contest. Join us for delicious gumbo and great fun for all ages.

504.329.4279 • www.gumbofestival.org

Chicken Sausage Gumbo

1 roasted fryer,
   boned and cut into bite-sized pieces
1 pound smoked sausage, cut cross-sectionally into 3/8-inch pieces and browned
1 cup all-purpose flour
¾ cup olive oil or butter
8 ounces (1 large) onion, small dice
6 ounces each celery (2 to 3 ribs) and bell pepper (1 medium), small dice
1 tablespoon minced garlic
1 pound okra, sliced cross sectionally (frozen is okay)
½ cup white wine
1 (28-ounce) can tomatoes, diced with juice
1 (6-ounce) can tomato sauce
1 teaspoon each dried basil, oregano, thyme
1 bay leaf
1 tablespoon salt
1 teaspoon each white, black and cayenne pepper
1 tablespoon Worcestershire sauce
1 teaspoon liquid smoke
1 pint chicken stock, or more after cooking, to adjust the texture to a thick soup consistency

Brown flour in a 400° oven approximately 45 minutes to a dark peanut butter color while preparing other ingredients. (As an alternative, the oil and flour can be mixed together to make a roux and stirred frequently over medium heat until it browns to chocolate color. This will take about 30 to 45 minutes). Sift browned flour and add to a heavy cast-iron Dutch oven, along with olive oil, over high heat. Stir well until uniform and hot and then add onions, celery and bell pepper. Cook over high heat 10 to 12 minutes, stirring occasionally, or until vegetable mixture becomes shiny and translucent. Add garlic and cook 1 to 2 minutes more. Add okra and continue cooking until okra begins to soften, about 5 to 7 minutes. Deglaze with wine, add tomato products, herbs, seasonings, chicken, sausage, and all remaining ingredients. Stir gumbo until all ingredients are uniformly distributed, bring to a boil, reduce heat and simmer 1½ hours, uncovered, stirring occasionally. Adjust gumbo texture, if necessary, and then adjust seasonings to taste. Serve over white rice with French bread.

Chef Ross Headlee, Louisiana Culinary Institute

Cajun Black-Eyed Pea Gumbo

2 tablespoons olive oil
1 pound smoked sausage, chopped
1 onion, chopped
1 green bell pepper, chopped
2 cups chopped celery
2 cups chicken broth
2 cups water
4 cans black-eyed peas
2 cans diced Rotel
1 can diced tomatoes
2 cloves garlic, finely chopped
2 tablespoons Cajun seasoning

Heat oil in a saucepan over medium heat; add sausage. Remove sausage and add onion, bell pepper and celery; continue to cook until vegetables are soft. Add broth, water, sausage, black-eyed peas, Rotel, diced tomatoes, garlic and Cajun seasoning. Bring to a boil, reduce heat to low, and simmer 45 minutes to an hour. Add more water or broth if gumbo is too thick.

CHRISTMAS PARADE AND GUMBO COOKOFF

Second Sunday in December • Morganza

Join us for live music in the streets from 10 am until the last person goes home. You'll enjoy craft and novelty booths, food booths, and gumbo galore. There are free photos with Santa Claus from 11 am to 1 pm. Gumbo judging begins at noon, and the parade starts at 2pm. There's fun for all ages including children's rides, carousel, rock climbing, and spacewalks. Come early and stay all day so you won't miss any of the fun.

225.694.3655

Veggie Gumbo

1 cup flour
1 cup oil
3 tablespoons butter
2 tablespoons minced garlic
2 cups chopped onion
2 cups chopped celery
2 cups chopped green bell pepper
2 cups diced tomatoes
2 cups chopped okra
2 cups chopped squash
1 can whole kernel corn
2 cans chicken broth
3 cans water
1 tablespoon hot sauce
2 tablespoons Cajun seasoning
Water to thin

Make a roux by cooking oil and flour in a skillet over medium-low heat until dark brown. Place in a large pot. Melt butter in skillet over medium heat. Add garlic and onion; cook until brown. Add to pot along with remaining ingredients. Cook over medium-high heat about 30 minutes. Serve hot with rice and French Bread.

WORLD CHAMPIONSHIP GUMBO COOKOFF

Second Weekend in October • New Iberia

The World Championship Gumbo Cookoff is held the second weekend in October in downtown New Iberia, LA. Enjoy live music Friday night and a Food Fest and Shopping Extravaganza on Saturday with music and special street events. Sunday is the "Battle of the Rouxs" with over seventy teams competing for the World's best gumbo. Bring the family for this fun-filled event. Sponsored by the Greater Iberia Chamber of Commerce and Tabasco.

337.364.1836 • www.iberiachamber.org

Ham & Okra Gumbo

1 cup flour
1 cup oil
1 pound cubed cooked ham
4 tablespoons butter
1 cup chopped onion
1 cup chopped celery
1 cup chopped green bell pepper

3 cans chicken broth
2 cans water
2 tablespoons hot sauce
Salt and pepper
½ tablespoon garlic powder
1 bag frozen chopped okra
1 can whole kernel corn

In a large pot, add flour and oil; cook over low heat until browned. In a skillet, brown ham; add to pot. Melt butter in same skillet over medium-high heat. Add onion, celery and bell pepper and cook until browned; add to pot along with remaining ingredients. Cook, covered, over medium heat about 30 minutes. Serve over cooked rice.

Duck Gumbo

4 duck breasts
1 cup cooking oil
1 cup flour
1 cup chopped onion
2 cloves garlic, minced

Tabasco, salt and red pepper
½ tablespoon white pepper
3 quarts water, boiling
½ pound smoked sausage, sliced
Chopped green onion tops, optional

Rinse duck, cut into serving size pieces, and set aside. In a large stockpot, heat oil and flour, stirring constantly, until dark brown. Add onion and garlic; cook until tender. Add Tabasco, salt and red pepper to taste. Add white pepper, water and sausage. Cook over medium heat 45 minutes to 60 minutes. Add duck and continue cooking until tender. Serve over cooked rice.

Allen Parish, Oberlin

Shrimp & Okra Fire Gumbo

½ cup oil
½ cup flour
½ gallon water
4 cups chicken stock
4 chicken bouillon cubes
3 jalapeño peppers, minced
⅔ cup butter
2 pounds okra, sliced
1 large onion, chopped
1 green bell pepper, chopped
1 clove garlic, minced
2 tablespoons chopped parsley
1 can (about 12 ounces) chopped tomatoes
2 pounds shrimp, peeled

Combine oil and flour in a skillet; cook over medium-high heat until brown to make a roux. In a large pot combine roux, water, stock, bouillon cubes, and jalapeño peppers. In a saucepan, simmer butter until melted and add okra, onion and bell pepper; sauté. Add garlic and chopped parsley; cook 2 minutes. Add to pot along with tomatoes. Cook about 1 hour. Add shrimp and cook over medium heat for 30 minutes. Serve over cooked rice with a slice of French Bread.

Stephen Nash, Baton Rouge

SPICE & MUSIC FESTIVAL

First Weekend in June ⋄ Opelousas

The City of Opelousas boasts a rich and colorful culture like no other. Designated as the Zydeco Capital of the World and the Spice Capital of Louisiana, the Spice & Music Festival, held the first weekend in June, features the best in Cajun and Zydeco music as well as mouth watering Cajun and Creole food. Held in downtown Opelousas in the center of a National Historic Register, the festival offers visitors and locals a taste of Southwest Louisiana heritage and of course, lots of spice!

337.948.5227 ⋄ www.cityofopelousas.com

Sherrie's Easy Seafood Gumbo (no roux)

Cooking oil
3 cups chopped okra
Salt and pepper
1 medium onion, finely chopped
2 to 4 cloves garlic, finely chopped
1 bell pepper, finely chopped
Italian herbs
Gumbo Filé
1 can peeled tomatoes, chopped
5 whole bay leaves
1 small can tomato paste
1 pound lump crabmeat
2 pounds peeled shrimp

When Sherrie is longing for the tastes of home–New Orleans–she always whips up a pot of her gumbo in her New York home. "It's done with no roux, but it has plenty or New Orleans flavor."

Coat bottom of a pot with cooking oil (I use olive oil). Add okra, sprinkle with salt and cook over medium heat until okra is no longer roping. Add a little water, cover and cook a few minutes until tender. Coat bottom of a separate large pot with cooking oil. Cook onions, garlic, bell pepper, Italian herbs, and filé until slightly brown and vegetables are tender. If you need more moisture, add a little juice from peeled tomatoes. Add okra, tomatoes, bay leaves and a little water. Mix thoroughly, cover, and cook over medium to medium-low heat about 15 minutes. Add tomato paste; stir. Add 1 cup water, and continue cooking over medium heat. Stir and add another cup water every 15 minutes (or as needed) for 1 hour. Add peeled shrimp, cook another 20 minutes. Add crabmeat and cook another 15 minutes.

Sherrie Henne, Now a New York Cajun

Seafood Gumbo with Roux

Roux:

1 cup flour
1 cup vegetable oil
2 onions, chopped
Chopped garlic to taste

In a 10-inch iron frying pan (or equivalent), add flour and oil. Set on low flame; stir constantly with a wooden paddle until the roux looks like dark chocolate. Turn off fire. (If you are in a hurry, you can use Savoie's Real Cajun Old Fashioned Dark Roux; although it is not a good as making your own.) Add onions and garlic. Use finished roux for your dish of choice—shrimp stew, chicken fricassee, or seafood gumbo.

Seafood Gumbo:

2 pounds cut okra
Olive Oil
Roux
1 pound crabmeat
2 pounds shrimp
1 can Rotel
1 can chopped tomatoes
½ cup chopped parsley
½ cup chopped shallots
2 to 4 cups prepared rice

Place okra (may be frozen) on cookie sheet, sprinkle with a small amount of olive oil, and cook at 350° for 20 to 25 minutes. In a heavy 8-quart pot, bring ½ gallon water (8 cups) to a boil (feel free to use more or less water depending on your desired consistency). Add Roux, reduce heat, and simmer about 1 hour. Add okra; cook an additional 20 minutes. Add crabmeat, shrimp, Rotel and chopped tomatoes. Cook 10 to 15 minutes. Add parsley and shallots; stir. Serve over rice.

Dutch & Kay Kihnemann

Easy Crawfish Gumbo

1½ pounds crawfish meat
10 cups chicken broth
1 package Creole or Cajun gumbo mix
2 pounds smoked sausage, sliced and browned
1 to 2 small onions, diced
1 small green bell pepper, diced
¼ cup chopped fresh parsley
1 to 2 cans okra gumbo
1 to 2 cans corn, drained
1 cup rice

Rinse crawfish; set aside to drain. Add chicken broth and gumbo mix to a large pot; simmer. Add remaining ingredients, except rice, and cook over low to medium heat for 1 hour. Stir in crawfish; add water, if needed. Add rice and cook until rice is done.

Combo Gumbo

¼ cup flour
3 tablespoons vegetable oil
2 medium onions, chopped
2 cups chopped celery
2 large green bell peppers, chopped
2 cloves garlic, minced
4 cups chicken broth
2 cans whole tomatoes with juice
1 package frozen sliced okra
1 bay leaf
1 tablespoon hot sauce
¾ pound cooked chicken
½ pound shrimp, peeled and deveined

Combine flour and oil in a large pot; cook over low heat until mixture turns brown. Add onions, celery, bell pepper and garlic; cook 5 minutes or until vegetables are tender. Gradually add broth. Stir in tomatoes, okra, bay leaf and hot sauce; bring to a boil. Add chicken and shrimp; cook 3 to 5 minutes or until shrimp turn pink. Remove bay leaf before serving. Serve with cooked rice.

Garlic Roux Chicken Sausage Gumbo

1 tablespoon minced garlic
1 cup oil
1 cup flour
3 cups cubed chicken
2 pounds andouille sausage, cut into ½-inch pieces
2 large onions, chopped
2 bell peppers, chopped
4 ribs celery, chopped
4 quarts chicken stock
2 bay leaves
3 teaspoons Creole seasoning
1 teaspoon thyme
Salt and pepper to taste
1 bunch scallions (tops only), chopped
⅔ cup fresh chopped parsley

In a large pot, heat garlic in oil; stir in flour. Cook, stirring constantly, until medium to dark brown. In a skillet, brown the chicken and sausage with onion, bell pepper, and celery. Drain excess fat; add to roux. Add remaining ingredients, bring to a boil and reduce heat. Simmer on low for 1 hour.

Baked Gumbo

1 cup plus
  1 tablespoon olive oil, divided
1 cup skinless, boneless chicken breast halves, chopped
½ pound pork sausage links, thinly sliced
1 cup all-purpose flour
1½ tablespoons minced garlic
1 can chicken broth
1 (12-fluid-ounce) can or bottle beer
2 stalks celery, diced
1 can diced tomatoes
1 sweet onion, sliced
1 (10-ounce) can diced tomatoes with green chile peppers, with liquid
1 tablespoon chopped fresh red chile peppers
1 bunch fresh parsley, chopped
¼ cup Cajun seasoning
½ pound shrimp, peeled and deveined

Heat 1 tablespoon oil in a large saucepan over medium-high heat; add chicken and cook until done. Stir in sausage, and cook until evenly browned. In a large, heavy saucepan over medium heat, blend 1 cup olive oil and flour to create a roux. Add remaining ingredients, except shrimp, plus chicken and sausage. Cook 15 minutes. Pour into a large casserole dish and stir in shrimp. Bake at 350° for 30 minutes.

Crabmeat Etouffée

2 pounds crabmeat
¼ cup vegetable oil
2 onions, chopped
1 cup chopped celery
½ cup diced green bell pepper
2 large cloves garlic, minced
2 bay leaves
½ cup clam juice
1 cup water
1 tablespoon flour
2 tablespoons finely chopped fresh parsley
3 tablespoons chopped green onion
Salt, black pepper, and cayenne pepper to taste

Flake crabmeat and set aside. Heat oil in a large skillet. Add onion, celery, and bell pepper; sauté over medium-high heat until soft. Add garlic and bay leaves; reduce heat. Stir in clam juice, water, and flour. Add crabmeat, parsley, and green onions. Cook 5 minutes, or until mixture is heated thoroughly. Add salt, black pepper, and cayenne pepper to taste. Remove bay leaves before serving. Serve over rice.

ETOUFFEE FESTIVAL

Last full weekend in April • Arnaudville

Our yearly Etouffée Festival is a fund raiser for St. John Francis Regis Catholic Church. There is a pageant the weekend before the festival. Friday through Sunday you will enjoy lots of good music, beer and daiquiris, etouffée, bar-b-que, bingo, a silent auction, mayor's cook-off, and much more. This is a fun event for people of all ages.

337.754.5912

24th Annual
Etouffée Festival
2009
Benefit of
St. John Francis Regis
Catholic Church

Friday, April 24
5:00 pm
until Midnight

Saturday, April 25
11:00 am
until Midnight

Sunday, April 26
11:00 am
until 5:00 pm

Little Flower School Grounds
Main Street • Arnaudville
337-754-5912
email: johnfrancisregis@hotmail.com

Shrimp Creole

4 tablespoons plus
  1 stick butter, divided
1 large onion, chopped
1 large green bell pepper, chopped
4 ribs celery, chopped
3 tablespoons minced parsley
4 cloves garlic, minced
2 (16-ounce) cans tomatoes
¼ teaspoon thyme
2 bay leaves
1½ teaspoons paprika
Salt and cayenne pepper to taste
2 tablespoons cornstarch
4 cups raw shrimp, peeled

Melt 4 tablespoons butter and sauté the next 5 ingredients until they become limp. Chop tomatoes in blender 1 to 2 seconds. Add tomatoes to sautéed mixture. Add thyme, bay leaves, paprika, salt and cayenne pepper; simmer over low heat 20 minutes, stirring occasionally. Mix cornstarch in ½ cup water and blend into the sauce at the end of the 20 minutes. In another pan, melt 1 stick butter and sauté shrimp until very pink. Add shrimp, along with all liquid to other mixture and blend well. Cook over low heat for another 40 to 50 minutes. You may have to add a little water along the way to keep the right consistency. Serve over fluffy hot rice.

Minnie Popich, Placquemines Parish

Vegetables & Other Side Dishes

Angie's Mock Shoe (MAQUE CHOUX)

2 medium red bell peppers, halved lengthwise
2 cans whole kernel corn
2 tablespoons butter or margarine, divided
2 tablespoons vegetable oil
1 small onion, finely chopped
1 tablespoon sugar
½ teaspoon Tabasco
½ cup chicken broth
⅓ cup heavy cream
1 egg, lightly beaten

This is my version of Maque Choux as I learned it from my Mom—it was one of my Dad's favorites.

Steam pepper halves about 8 minutes. Drain corn and set aside. In a medium skillet, heat 1 tablespoon butter with 2 tablespoons oil. Add corn, onion, sugar and Tabasco. Cook until corn is almost tender and starts to form a crust on bottom of pan. Gradually stir in broth, scraping up bits on bottom of pan. Stir in remaining 1 tablespoon butter and cream. Cook 5 minutes longer or until almost all liquid evaporates; stir frequently. Remove skillet from heat. Add egg; stir 1 minute or until egg is cooked. Serve in red pepper halves.

Angie Conner & Family, Lake Charles

Corn Maque Choux

4 ounces (¼ cup) olive oil
8 ounces (1 cup) finely chopped onion
6 ounces (¾ cup) finely chopped bell pepper
4 ounces (½ cup) finely chopped celery
2 tablespoons minced garlic
2 ounces white wine
1 teaspoon each dried basil, thyme and oregano
2 bay leaves
1 can Rotel, drained
6 ounces tomato sauce
2 tablespoons Worcestershire sauce
1 very large can (12 cups) corn with juice
Salt, pepper, cayenne to taste

Over high heat in a heavy saucepan, heat olive oil; add onions, bell pepper and celery and sweat until translucent, about 2 to 3 minutes, stirring occasionally. Add garlic and cook 1 minute more. Add wine and herbs. Reduce wine mixture slightly and Rotel, tomato sauce and Worcestershire. Simmer 20 to 30 minutes, stirring occasionally. Add corn and continue simmering 10 minutes. Adjust seasoning and serve hot.

Chef Ross Headlee, Louisiana Culinary Institute

Cajun Fried Corn

3 cans whole kernel corn
6 slices bacon
½ cup chopped onion
½ cup milk
1 teaspoon salt
1 teaspoon black pepper
1 jalapeño pepper, chopped
2 dashes hot sauce
Red pepper flakes
¼ cup chopped pecans
Pinch sugar

Drain corn and set aside. In a large skillet, cook bacon until crisp; drain on a paper towel. Reserve ¼ teaspoon drippings in the skillet; add corn and onion. Cook over medium heat until well browned. Add milk and seasonings, stirring until well mixed. When liquid is almost cooked off, add pecans and a pinch of sugar.

Dale Harper

LOUISIANA CORN FESTIVAL

Second full weekend in June • Bunkie

Aw Shucks! The Louisiana Corn Festival is held the second full weekend in June. It is a three day, family fun event and it is free to attend. Opening Ceremony is Friday, and the fun begins with the children's parade. There is a large carnival, arts & crafts and food vendors with something for everyone. Our city-wide parade is on Saturday at 11:00 am, after that the games begin. Get ready to compete in the corn eating, shucking and cooking contests. For sports-minded individuals, we have softball games with 16 teams competing and pirogue races on the bayou. The music doesn't stop with live bands and a street dance both nights. On Sunday is our talent competition and battle of the bands. So join us for a shucking good time.

800.833.4195 • bunkie.org

Hominy Casserole

3 cans hominy with peppers
1 can cream of mushroom soup
1 can nacho cheese soup
1 cup shredded Cheddar cheese

Drain hominy and mix with both soups. Pour into casserole dish. Cover with cheese. Heat in 350° oven until bubbly and hot.

Nannette Bryant, Blanchard
"Something New in 92"
Poke Salad Festival Official Cookbook

THE ANNUAL POKE SALAD FESTIVAL

2nd Saturday in May • Blanchard

The Poke Salad Festival has been held the 2nd Saturday in May for the past 34 years in Blanchard Louisiana, and is hosted by The Annual Poke Salad Festival Association. Leading up to the festival we have a treasure hunt, a store front decoration contest, a youth concert, and a 3-day carnival. Saturday's festivities feature a hometown parade, arts, crafts, food, and music starting at 10:00 am and ending with a street dance, now at the Poke Salad Pavilion, all on the festival grounds in Blanchard. For complete information on each year's events, please check our web page at www.PokeSaladFestival.com.

318.309.2647 or 318.929.7574 • www.PokeSaladFestival.com

Spicy Vegetable Bake

1 can Rotel
1 bag mixed frozen vegetables
½ cup chopped pecans or almonds
Cajun seasoning
Dash hot sauce
Salt and pepper
Parmesean cheese

Combine all ingredients in glass baking dish. Cover and bake at 350° for 30 to 45 minutes. The frozen vegetables will add plenty of steam. Serve hot over rice. (For a creamy version, I sometimes stir in a can of cream of mushroom soup.)

The Williamson Family, Lafayette

Bacon Scalloped Potatoes

5 strips bacon
1 onion, chopped
1 tablespoon butter
4 potatoes, peeled and sliced
1 can cream of mushroom
⅔ cup milk
Salt and pepper

In a large heavy skillet, cook bacon; set aside to cool. In the same skillet, cook onion in butter until tender. Stir in potatoes, soup, milk, salt and pepper. Bring to a boil, reduce heat, cover and simmer until potatoes are tender, 10 to 20 minutes. Crumbled bacon and sprinkle on top before serving. (You can remove from skillet and bake at 350° instead of finishing in the skillet, if desired.)

Grilled Creole Vegetables

3 to 4 large potatoes
1 large onion
1 bell peppers
2 carrots
1 can water chestnuts
1 teaspoon rosemary
1 teaspoon thyme
1 teaspoon garlic powder
1 teaspoon chili powder
½ teaspoon cayenne pepper

Wash and slice all vegetables. Grease 4 large sheets of tin foil with cooking spray. Place ½ of the vegetables on 1 sheet of foil and ½ on another. Sprinkle herbs over vegetables, use as much or as little as you like. Place the remaining foil pieces top of the vegetables and tightly roll up each edge so the vegetables cannot fall out. Grill until vegetable are tender, about 10 to 15 minutes on each side.

Chive Mashed Potatoes

½ tablespoon minced garlic
4 tablespoons chopped chives
1 tablespoon minced onion
Olive oil
4 cups peeled, diced russet potatoes
Salt and pepper
1 cup heavy cream
4 tablespoons unsalted butter

In a skillet, cook minced garlic, chives and onions in some olive oil. In a pot, boil potatoes in water to cover seasoned with salt and pepper to taste. Boil until potatoes are soft; drain. Add cream, cooked garlic mixture, and stir. Add butter and beat with mixer until fluffy. Serve hot.

Candied Sweet Potatoes

**8 to 10 sweet potatoes,
 peeled and cut**
2 cups sugar
½ stick butter

Peel potatoes, cut lengthwise. Boil until tender. Mix sugar and cinnamon; set aside. Drain potatoes, add sugar mixture and butter. Cook until a thick syrup forms over sweet potatoes.

In Memory of Daisy Mae Watkins, Starks

Holy Trinity Mardi Gras Potatoes

6 russet potatoes, cubed
1 onion, chopped
1 green bell pepper, chopped
1 cup chopped celery
1 stick butter
Minced garlic to taste
Shredded cheese

Clean and cube potatoes; cover with water, add a pinch of salt, and boil until tender. While potatoes cook, heat onion, bell pepper, celery, butter, and garlic in a skillet over medium heat. When potatoes are soft, drain and roughly mash (do not cream). Stir in sautéed items. Spoon into a baking dish and bake at 350° for 25 minutes. Cover in cheese and serve.

Sweet Potato Casserole

3 cups sweet potatoes
   (about 5 medium-large)
½ cup butter, softened
½ cup sugar
2 eggs
1 teaspoon vanilla
⅓ cup evaporated milk
Topping:
1½ cups brown sugar
¾ cup flour
1½ cups chopped pecans
½ cup melted butter

Any time we have a family get-together or a party with friends, they don't ask what I am bringing, they just say "Bring your sweet potato casserole." I also bring copies of the recipe as someone always asks for it. I believe that baking the potatoes enhances the flavor and it is not as sweet as some casseroles I've tried.

Bake and peel potatoes; mash with butter. Add sugar, eggs, vanilla and milk. Mix well and pour into a 9x13-inch greased baking dish. Combine dry ingredients for Topping, then stir in melted butter. Sprinkle over top of potato mixture. Bake at 350° for 25 minutes. Serves 8 to 10.

Mary Pringle, Forest Hill

YAMBILEE

Last Full Weekend in October • Opelousas

THE SWEET GOLDEN YAM (sweet potato) has been something to celebrate ever since the Frenchmen, who established the first settlement here in 1760, discovered the native Indians eating sweet potatoes. The Yambilee Festival starts on the Thursday before the last full weekend of October and continues throughout the weekend. There are fun things for people of all ages including live music, cooked yam competition, yam-i-mal competition, carnival, talent competition, parade, food and crafts booth and so much more. Join us, And we guarantee, You'll have a Yam-Good-Time!

337.948.8845 • www.yambilee.com

Home-Style Collard Greens

3 pounds collard greens, rinsed and cut
1 large piece of pork fat back (or 3 slices bacon, chopped)
¼ cup bacon drippings
1 beef bouillon cube
1 medium onion, chopped
2 garlic cloves, minced
2 tablespoons cider vinegar
2 teaspoons sugar
1/2 teaspoon crushed red pepper
3 cups water
Salt and pepper to taste

Clean and rinse greens; set aside. In a large pot, combine fat back, bacon drippings and onion; cover over low heat until dripping are melted. Add garlic, sugar, red pepper and water. Add collards, salt and pepper. Stir well and simmer on low until greens are soft, at least 30 minutes.

FRENCH FOOD FESTIVAL

Last Full Weekend in October • Bayou Lafourche

The French Food Festival features over 20 local specialty dishes plus dancing and music. Experience the essence of life on Bayou Lafourche with folklife demonstrations offering everyone the chance to learn about Cajun living -- boat building, cooking, music and more. More than just a food festival, the French Food Festival includes an old-fashioned carnival midway, complete with games, rides, and cotton candy. Join us for family fun for all ages and experience more than 200 years of a legacy rich with traditions, legends, and a distinctive way of life.

985.693.7355 • www.bayoucivicclub.org

Poke Salad Casserole

1 can cream of mushroom soup
2 eggs, separated
1 (8-ounce) package cream cheese, softened
2 to 3 cups poke salad, cooked and drained
4 tablespoons Parmesan cheese
1 can French fried onion rings
½ cup grated cheese (or to taste), optional

Heat soup. Beat egg yolks, set aside. Mash cream cheese. Add egg yolks and cream choose to hot soup. Add poke salad, beaten egg whites, and Parmesan cheese. Put in casserole; top with onion rings and add a little cheese on top, if desired. Bake at 350° for 35 to 45 minutes.

Artelia McIntosh

Brooke's Spinach Casserole

1 package Uncle Ben's Wild Rice
1 small can mushrooms, drained
1 teaspoon yellow mustard
2¼ cups water
1 (10-ounce) package frozen spinach
¾ cup chopped onion
2 tablespoons butter
1 (8-ounce) package cream cheese

Combine rice, seasoning packet, mushrooms and mustard in a baking dish; set aside. Bring water, spinach, onion and butter to a boil in saucepan. Pour over rice and bake, covered, at 350° for 30 minutes. Remove from oven, and stir in cream cheese. Bake another 10 to 15 minutes, uncovered. Serve warm.

Kathleen Robinson from the "Robinson & Stirling Family Recipe Collection"

Bacon Fried Cabbage

6 slices bacon
1 head cabbage, sliced
2 tablespoons apple cider vinegar
1 tablespoon sugar
Salt and pepper to taste

Fry bacon in large skillet over medium heat until crispy. Remove bacon from skillet and set aside to drain. Add cabbage to skillet and fry in drippings. Add vinegar, sugar and seasonings. Cook 10 to 15 minutes. Crumble reserved bacon, stir into cabbage, and serve immediately.

Broccoli Bacon Casserole

2 cans cream of mushroom soup
1 pound Velveeta cubed
1½ cups Minute Rice
1 cup chopped pecans
1 cup cooked and crumbled bacon
1 (16-ounce) bag frozen broccoli cuts

Mix all together. Spread in a casserole dish. Cover with aluminum foil and bake at 350° for 30 minutes. Uncover, stir and bake another 5 minutes.

Squash Casserole

3 to 4 cups cooked squash
1 onion, finely chopped
1 can cream of mushroom soup
2 eggs, beaten
1 cup grated or cubed cheese
2 cups crushed Ritz or Saltine Crackers, divided
¼ cup butter

Cook squash and onion. Add soup, eggs, cheese, and 1 cup cracker crumbs. Pour into casserole dish. Top with additional 1 cup cracker crumbs and dot with butter. Bake at 350° for 30 minutes or until brown.

Jean Hall

Louisiana is known as the Pelican State

© Sherri Klein • bigstockphoto.com

MawMaw Mary's Artichoke Leaves

1¼ pounds fresh medium shrimp with heads
Zatarain's crab and shrimp boil (liquid or powder)
1 fresh artichoke
¾ can olive oil
4 tablespoons butter or margarine
1 medium onion, chopped fine
2 cups finely chopped green onion, tops and bottoms
⅔ cup very finely chopped garlic
1 (14-ounce) can artichoke hearts, finely chopped, liquid reserved
2 cups Italian breadcrumbs
1 cup shredded Romano cheese
1 tablespoon shredded or finely grated Parmesan cheese
1 tablespoon ground paprika

Rinse shrimp and cook in water seasoned according to package directions with crab boil; drain. Remove heads and peel shrimp; refrigerate. Boil fresh artichoke in clean water until leaves pull off easily, about 30 minutes. Drain and let cool. Remove and refrigerate leaves (about 45). Scoop out and discard fuzzy choke over the heart. Chop heart and tender center of stem; refrigerate if prepared ahead. Heat olive oil and butter in a very large skillet. Add onions, green onions and garlic. Cook over high heat until clear and tender, about 8 to 10 minutes, stirring occasionally. Add canned artichokes, liquid from can and reserved artichoke heart and stem. Thoroughly mix in breadcrumbs, then cheeses. Remove from heat. Spoon about one heaping teaspoon of stuffing onto bottom part of each artichoke leaf. Use all stuffing. Sprinkle leaves lightly with paprika and top each with a shrimp; if needed, cut larger shrimp in half to have enough for all leaves. Serve immediately or cover and refrigerate. (Can be prepared up to two days ahead; bring to room temperature or lightly heat before serving.)

Leslie Hoffmann, Metairie (in memory of Mary Marcotte)

Fried Okra

3 (10-ounce) packages frozen okra
2 eggs, beaten
1 tablespoon Worcestershire sauce
1 teaspoon garlic salt
1 teaspoon hot sauce
White cornmeal
Vegetable oil
Salt
Cajun Seasoning

Allow okra to thaw and drain. If using whole okra, cut and discard ends then slice. In large saucepan, cook okra in 1 inch boiling water about 8 minutes; drain. In small bowl, beat together eggs, Worcestershire sauce, garlic salt and hot sauce. Dip okra first into egg mixture then into cornmeal to cover. Fry in hot oil 2 to 3 minutes or until golden. Drain on paper towels. Sprinkle with salt and Cajun seasoning to taste. Serve hot.

Red 'n' Green

¼ cup (½ stick) butter
2 tablespoons olive oil
2 cups chopped celery
2 onions, chopped
2 pounds okra, chopped
2 cans whole tomatoes, broken up
½ pound andouille sausage
Creole seasoning
Salt and freshly ground black pepper, to taste
1 can whole-kernel corn, optional

This is an okra and tomato dish we always called "Red 'n' Green. It's a common dish around Louisiana and the South. We just had a fun name for it!

Heat butter and olive oil in a large pot over medium heat. Add celery and onions, and cook 5 minutes or until translucent. Add okra, tomatoes, sausage and Creole seasoning to taste. Cover and cook over medium heat at least 45 minutes. A can of whole-kernel corn can be added, if desired.

Bobby Landry, New Orleans

TOMATO FESTIVAL

May • Chalmette

The Tomato Festival is a St. Bernard Tradition and has been for the past 58 years. Sponsored by Our Lady of Prompt Succor School, this family oriented event features live entertainment, a baby contest, pageant, amusement rides, and, of course, lots of great food. Join us for lots of fun for people of all ages.

504.271.2953 • www.olpsschool.org

Okra & Bacon Casserole

1½ pounds young, fresh okra
3 large tomatoes, chopped
1 onion, chopped
1 green bell pepper, chopped
2 teaspoons hot sauce
Salt and pepper to taste
Garlic powder to taste
8 slices bacon, uncooked

Slice okra into thin rounds. In greased 2½-quart casserole, combine okra, tomatoes, onion, bell pepper and hot sauce. Sprinkle with salt, pepper and garlic powder. Place bacon on top. Bake, uncovered, at 350° for 1½ hours, or until okra is tender.

Okra and Tomatoes with Sausage

1 pound okra
½ cup chopped green bell pepper
½ cup chopped onion
1 rib celery, chopped
6 tomatoes, peeled and chopped
½ pound link sausage, cut into bit-size pieces

Slice okra and combine with pepper, onions and celery; sauté. Add tomatoes and continue to cook. Add sausage. Lightly fry vegetables and sausage, but do not brown. Add a little water and simmer 1 hour to tenderize sausage. Serve over rice.

Virginia Smith, Monroe

Renee's Homemade Macaroni and Cheese

1 (8-ounce) package macaroni
4 tablespoons butter
4 tablespoons flour
½ teaspoon salt
Freshly ground black pepper, to taste
1 cup milk
1 cup cream
2 cups good-quality shredded Cheddar cheese
1 can green chiles and diced tomatoes
½ cup buttered breadcrumbs

Cook and drain macaroni according to directions. In a large saucepan, melt butter and add flour mixed with salt and pepper, stir until blended. Add milk and cream. Mix well and simmer about 15 minutes. Reduce heat. Add cheese little by little and stir until melted. Stir in tomatoes and pour into an oven-safe dish. Coat with breadcrumbs. Bake at 375° until golden brown.

Renee Hebert & Family, Lafayette

INTERNATIONAL RICE FESTIVAL

3rd weekend in October • Crowley

The International Rice Festival is one of the oldest and largest agricultural festivals in the South. Since the inauguration of the first festival on October 5, 1937, millions have attended the annual event. The International Rice Festival calls attention to the importance of rice as a food and to emphasize its place in the world's economic picture. Always held the third weekend in October, the Festival takes place in the downtown area of Crowley and is one of the few festivals free to the public. The celebration would not be possible without contributions from industries, businesses, and individuals. A very special recognition must be given to the many volunteers who have given of their time and talents to make this event the success that it is each year.

337-783-3067 • www.ricefestival.com

Baked Macaroni and Cheese

1 (8-ounce) package pasta, any shape
2 cups grated sharp Cheddar cheese, divided
¼ cup butter or margarine
¼ cup flour
2 cups milk
1 small package Velveeta cheese
Salt and pepper to taste

This is a family favorite handed down from my mother. I make it for every holiday.

Cook pasta according to package directions. Drain. Pour into baking dish. Add ½ cup cheese and mix well. In saucepan, melt butter. Remove from heat and blend in flour. Return to heat. Gradually stir in milk. Continue stirring frequently. Cut up Velveeta cheese and add to pan. Bring to a boil. Simmer on low heat until cheese is melted. Pour over macaroni. Mix well. Top with remaining grated cheese. Bake in 375° oven about 10 to 15 minutes or until cheese is melted.

Starr Puipuro, Metairie

BEAUREGARD WATERMELON FESTIVAL

Last Weekend in June • DeRidder

The Beauregard Watermelon Festival is always held the last weekend of June. Beauregard Parish, Home of the original Sugartown Watermelon is cherished amongst watermelon lovers for over a century for their sugar sweet watermelons. Join us for a fun-filled weekend with events like a Watermelon Eating Contest, Seed Spitting Contest, Carving Contest, Growers Contest along with amusement rides, yard art, Cajun music, farmers market, bluegrass music, and more. There is fun for all ages at this super summer event.

1.800.738.5534 • www.beauparish.org

Stuffed & Covered Pasta

18 to 20 large macaroni shells
1 pound ricotta cheese
1 egg, beaten
1½ cups shredded mozzarella cheese, divided
¼ cup Parmesan cheese
½ cup chopped parsley
½ teaspoon basil
½ teaspoon oregano
½ pound smoked sausage, finely chopped
½ pound salad shrimp
1 jar spaghetti sauce
⅓ cup water

Prepare shells according to package directions. Combine ricotta cheese and egg. Add 1 cup Mozzarella, Parmesan cheese, parsley, basil and oregano. Stir in sausage and shrimp. Combine spaghetti sauce and water in small bowl. Put ¾ cup sauce in bottom of baking dish. Fill shells with mixture and place in pan. Pour remaining sauce over top. Bake 35 minutes or until stuffed shells are heated through and cheese melts. Top with remaining ½ cup mozzarella cheese and broil until golden.

The Thompson Family, New Orleans

Angel Hair Pasta with Pink Cream Sauce

3 tablespoons butter
1 small onion, finely chopped
1 cup white wine
2½ cups chicken broth
1 (14½-ounce) can stewed or diced tomatoes
1 cup half & half
½ cup heavy cream
Salt and pepper to taste
1 pound Angel hair pasta, cooked and drained
½ cup freshly grated Romano or Parmesan cheese

Melt butter in saucepan. Add onions and sauté until almost brown, about 8 to 10 minutes. Add wine and bring to a boil. Reduce liquid to about 3 tablespoons. Add chicken broth. Boil and reduce liquid to ½ cup. In food processor, puree tomatoes. Add tomatoes to onion mixture and bring to a boil. Reduce to slow simmer and cook 30 minutes. Add both creams. Slowly simmer 10 minutes, stirring frequently. Season with salt and pepper. Toss gently over heated pasta and serve immediately with grated cheese on the side.

Jill Carney, Baton Rouge

White Beans & Rice

¼ cup vegetable oil
1 to 2 onions, chopped
1 pound cubed ham
1 pound white beans

Heat vegetable oil in saucepan; sauté onions until tender. Add ham and cook about 15 minutes. Add beans. Pour in water until beans are covered by an inch. Boil until beans are soft. Serve over cooked rice.

Kyle LaBlanc www.crawdads.net

Meaty Black-Eyed Peas

1 pound black-eyed peas
4 cups water
1 medium onion, quartered
½ teaspoon salt
¼ teaspoon pepper
2 polish sausages
½ cup chopped bacon
¼ teaspoon dried red pepper, optional

Wash black-eyed peas. Place in slow cooker or, if you wish to cook them on the top of the stove, a large Dutch oven. Add remaining ingredients. Set slow cooker to high (or simmer on stove) and cook 3 to 4 hours.

Hot Sausage Black-Eyed Pea Casserole

1 pound ground hot sausage, browned
1 tablespoon oil
1 purple onion, chopped
⅔ cup diced celery
1 red cayenne pepper, chopped
1½ pounds okra, ½-inch slices
2 cans black eyed peas, drained and rinsed
1 can diced tomatoes
2 tablespoons tomato paste
1 or 2 teaspoons crushed red chili flakes
1 cup water

Combine all ingredients in a covered baking dish and bake at 350° for 30 minutes.

Ben & Linda Campbell, LSU Football Fans

Ole Fashioned Hoppin' John

1 pound dried black-eyed peas,
   cleaned and rinsed
1 (10-ounce) cut ham hock
1 large onion, finely chopped
½ teaspoon dried hot red-pepper flakes
9 cups water
2 cups long-grain rice

Bring all ingredients, except rice, to a boil in a large heavy pot. Skim any foam off the top, then simmer, covered, for about 30 minutes. Transfer ham hock to a cutting board; cut away any skin from ham hock and chop meat, discarding bone if any. Transfer 4 cups peas and 4 cups cooking liquid to a heavy medium-sized pot. (Remaining peas and liquid can be refrigerated or frozen for a later use.) Stir rice and ham into smaller pot of peas with 1½ tablespoons salt and ½ teaspoon pepper. Bring to a rolling boil. Stir then simmer, tightly covered, over very low heat until rice is tender and liquid is gone. Remove from heat and allow to rest 5 minutes before serving.

Dale Harper

Reunion Baked Beans

1½ pounds ground meat
1 large onion, chopped
1 bell pepper, chopped
2 ribs celery, chopped
1 large (46-ounce) can Pork & Beans, drained
1 small can tomato sauce
½ cup shredded cheese or 4 slices of cheese cut in half for topping

In iron skillet, brown ground meat, onion, bell pepper, and celery; drain. Combine meat mixture with beans and tomato sauce. Pour in baking dish. Bake at 325° for 40 to 45 minutes; cover with cheese the last 10 minutes of cook time. Don't over cook—needs to be moist.

In memory of Daisy Mae Watkins, Starks

Dutch Green Beans

12 slices bacon
1 large onion, chopped
½ cup sugar
½ cup vinegar
¼ cup mustard
4 cans whole green beans, drained

Fry bacon, remove from pan, cool, crumble and reserve. Sauté onions in bacon drippings, then add sugar, vinegar, mustard, and beans; stir. Top with reserved bacon. Cover and cook over low heat for 2 hours.

Evelyn Watkins White, Starks

Meat

Creole Steaks & Shrimp

4 steaks, your choice of cut
16 (or more) large shrimp, peeled and deveined
2 tablespoons paprika
2 tablespoons salt
2 tablespoons garlic powder
1 tablespoon black pepper
1 tablespoon onion powder
1 tablespoon cayenne powder
1 tablespoon oregano
1 tablespoon thyme

Combine seasonings and evenly coat steaks and shrimp in a baking dish. Cover and chill about 30 minutes. Grill or pan-cook steaks to desired doneness. Before steaks are done, cook shrimp alongside on grill or in pan. Serve steaks topped with shrimp.

Grilled T-Bone Steak with Cucumber Sauce

Steaks:

2 to 4 T-Bone steaks
1 cup orange juice
⅓ cup Italian Dressing

Cucumber Sauce:

1 cucumber peeled, deseeded and grated
1 cup plain low-fat yogurt
3 tablespoons mayo
2 tablespoons olive oil
1 tablespoon minced celery (optional)
1 teaspoon salt
1 teaspoon dillweed
1 teaspoon apple cider vinegar
1 teaspoon minced garlic

Marinate meat in orange juice and Italian dressing for 2 hours or overnight. Combine Cucumber Sauce ingredients and mix well. Chill while steaks are grilling. Grill steaks until done. Server topped with sauce.

Pepper Jelly Grilled Rib-Eye Steak Open-Face

Rib-Eye steaks
Pepper jelly
French bread
Sliced onion
Sliced green bell pepper

Use quantities based on personal taste and how many people you are feeding. Marinate steaks in pepper jelly about 30 minutes before grilling. Grill over medium-high heat to desired doneness. Serve steak on top of a slice of grilled French bread topped with grilled onion and pepper slices.

The recipe is almost too easy! My dad made this steak all of the time and I thought it was the greatest ever. Rib-Eyes are my favorite, but any steak will do.

Beau "Lil Bo" Joshland

GRILLIN' IN THE PARK SOUTHWEST LA BARBEQUE CHAMPIONSHIP COOKOFF

April · New Iberia

This is the major fundraiser for the shepherd's food pantry. We have a day of barbeque cookoff, games with prizes for kids and many different fun and safety demonstrations. We do not allow alcohol because we want it to be a family event to show kids they can have fun and enjoyment without the use of alcohol. Some of the fun includes petting zoo, pony rides, fun jumps, craft booths, sweet booths and live music.

337.367.7388

Cajun Beef Pepper Steak

2 teaspoons Cajun seasoning, divided
1 pound boneless beef top sirloin steak, cut ¾-inch thick
2 medium green or red bell peppers, cut into quarters
2 teaspoons vegetable oil
1 (5½- to 8-ounce) package Cajun or Creole rice mix with seasonings

Press 1½ teaspoons seasoning blend evenly onto beef steak. Toss bell peppers with oil and remaining ½ teaspoon seasoning blend. Place steak in center of grill over medium, ash-covered coals, arrange bell peppers around steak. Grill, uncovered, 13 to 16 minutes for medium rare to medium doneness and peppers are tender, turning occasionally. Meanwhile prepare rice blend according to package directions, omitting oil or margarine. Carve steak into slices. Serve with peppers and rice.

Louisiana Beef Industry Council funded by the Beef Checkoff Program

Steak Chunks with Browned Garlic Butter Sauce

1 pound beef stew meat
¼ cup steak sauce
Salt, pepper and garlic powder to taste
¼ cup minced onion
Oil

Sauce:

¾ cup butter or margarine
2 cloves garlic, minced
2 tablespoons parsley, minced
1 tablespoon hot sauce

Coat meat in steak sauce, salt, pepper and garlic powder. Heat oil in skillet; cook meat and onions until meat is cooked through. In small saucepan, heat butter until half melted shaking pan constantly. Add garlic and cook 2 to 3 minutes or until butter is melted. Stir in parsley and hot sauce; cook 1 to 2 minutes longer. Serve meat over cooked rice covered with sauce.

Baked Tomato Veal

1 large egg, beaten
2 tablespoons water
⅔ cup dry breadcrumbs
⅓ cup flour
⅓ cup grated Parmesan cheese
1½ pounds veal cuts
Oil or butter for frying
2 cups spaghetti sauce
2 cups shredded mozzarella cheese

Mix egg and water in a bowl. In a separate bowl, combine breadcrumbs, flour and Parmesan cheese. Dip veal in egg mixture, then coat with breadcrumb mixture. Heat oil in 12-inch skillet over medium heat. Cook veal about 5 minutes, turning once, until light brown; drain. Place veal in a greased rectangular baking dish, overlapping slices slightly. Spoon half of the sauce over veal covering each piece. Sprinkle with 1 cup mozzarella cheese covering each piece. Repeat with remaining sauce and cheese. Bake uncovered at 350° for 30 minutes or until sauce is bubbly and cheese is light brown.

Pan Seared Veal

1 pound veal cutlets
½ cup all-purpose flour
2 tablespoons garlic powder
Cajun seasoning to taste
Salt and pepper to taste
¼ cup vegetable oil
1 stick butter
¼ cup dry white wine
2 tablespoons lemon juice
½ lemon, cut into 4 wedges
Parsley

Mix flour, garlic powder, Cajun seasoning, salt and pepper in a bowl. Coat veal with flour mixture. Heat oil in a skillet over medium-high heat. Cook veal until brown; remove from oil and keep warm. Drain oil; add butter, wine and lemon juice to skillet. Heat to boiling and boil until liquid is reduced by about half and mixture has thickened slightly. Pour over veal. Serve with garnished lemon wedges and parsley.

Skyline Shreveport

Skyline Shreveport © Eric McFarland

Barbecue Beef Brisket

1 beef brisket
Oil
2 teaspoons paprika
1 teaspoon ground black pepper, divided
1 tablespoon butter
1 medium onion, grated
1½ cups ketchup
1 tablespoon fresh lemon juice
1 tablespoon Worcestershire sauce
1 teaspoon hot pepper sauce

Rub brisket down with a light amount of oil. Combine paprika and ½ teaspoon black pepper; rub evenly over brisket. Put 2 cups mesquite wood chips in a bowl and cover with water. Chill brisket in fridge while wood chips soak for about 1 hour. Drain chips and place in foil or in a wood chip holder. Poke foil with fork to make a few holes in top. Place the chip container on grate to begin to heat up. Place brisket, fat side down, in 9x11½-inch disposable foil pan. Add ½ cup water. Place in center of grill over low heat or indirect heat and close grill cover. Cook 5 to 6 hours, turning brisket over every hour. Add water if needed. Reserve pan dripping. Skim fat from pan drippings; reserve 1 cup drippings. Melt butter in medium saucepan over medium heat. Add onion, cook until tender crisp. Add pan drippings, remaining ½ teaspoon black pepper, ketchup, lemon juice, Worcestershire sauce and hot pepper sauce. Bring to a boil and reduce heat. Serve with sliced brisket.

Northwest Louisiana Baked Beef Brisket

1 large beef brisket
1 tablespoon garlic powder
2 tablespoons celery seed
2 tablespoons black pepper
1 tablespoon seasoned salt
2 tablespoons liquid smoke
2 tablespoons Worcestershire sauce
2 tablespoons hot sauce

Place brisket in a large baking dish. In a small bowl, mix remaining ingredients and brush evenly over brisket. Cover and chill 1 hour or longer. Remove brisket from dish and wrap tightly in foil; return to dish and bake 4 hours at 275°. Check for doneness, cooking time may vary depending on brisket size. Allow to rest before slicing. Slice in thin slices and serve over French bread, if desired.

London Broil

3 pound London Broil
1 cup red wine
½ cup Italian dressing
Black pepper to taste
Minced garlic to taste

Combine all ingredients in a zip-lock bag. Place steak in bag, close and refrigerate about 2 hours. Grill to an internal temperature of 135°. (You want to cook this on a covered grill to keep the temps regulated.)

Daniel Williamson, New Orleans

Bayou Pot Roast

1 (2-pound) pork roast
3 tablespoons paprika
½ cup minced onion
¼ cup minced celery
½ tablespoon cayenne pepper
2 tablespoons garlic powder
2 teaspoons oregano
2 teaspoons thyme
1 teaspoon salt
1 teaspoon pepper
1 teaspoon cumin
1 teaspoon nutmeg

Combine all seasonings and rub well over all surfaces of roast. Place roast in shallow pan and roast in 350° oven about 90 minutes. Allow roast to rest 5 minutes before serving.

Diane's Famous Spaghetti Sauce

1 onion, diced
1 bell pepper, diced
1 celery stalk, diced
3 green onions, diced
3 garlic cloves, minced
¼ cup olive or vegetable oil
1 large (16-ounce) can whole tomatoes, smashed with fork
2 large (16-ounce) cans tomato sauce
Sugar to taste
2 pounds hamburger, optional

In heavy dutch oven, sauté onion, bell pepper, celery, green onions and garlic in oil. When onions are translucent (soft), add tomatoes and cook until tomatoes are cooked down and an oily film appears. Add tomato sauce and same amount of water. Bring to a boil. Continue to boil about 1 hour or until sauce is thick. Add sugar to taste (I like a sweet sauce). You can fry ground beef and add to sauce during the last 15 minutes of cooking. Serve over your favorite noodles with French bread on the side.

Christmas Celebration & Gumbo Cookoff, Morganza

Stuffed Bell Peppers

4 large bell peppers
1 pound lean chuck
1 tablespoon oil
2 slices bacon, chopped (optional)
1 medium onion, chopped
2 ribs celery, chopped
1 clove garlic, minced
1 teaspoon salt
½ teaspoon pepper
¼ teaspoon cayenne

¼ teaspoon each garlic powder and
   onion powder
½ cup cooked rice
½ cup Italian-style breadcrumbs
⅓ cup fresh Romano, grated (plus
   more for top)
¼ cup half & half
½ teaspoon lemon juice
½ teaspoon Worcestershire sauce

Cut tops off bell peppers and remove inner seeds. Split peppers in half length-wise. Parboil in salted water 6 to 8 minutes until just semi-tender. Drain on paper towels upside down. Brown chuck in a little oil until cooked through, about 5 minutes. Add bacon, onions and celery; cook over medium-high heat for 10 minutes. Turn off heat and add seasoning, cooked rice, breadcrumbs and ⅓ cup Romano; mix well. Blend in cream, lemon juice and Worcestershire. Stuff peppers with meat mixture and sprinkle tops with Romano cheese. Bake at 350° for 30 minutes in greased casserole dish.

Jill Carney, Baton Rouge

KIWANIS ST. MARTINVILLE PEPPER FESTIVAL

Third Sunday in October • St. Martinville

Kick up the heat and your heels at the Kiwanis Pepper Festival. Held under the historic Evangeline Oak, get ready for the scorching pepper eating contest, dance to red hot bands and enjoy the taste-temping local cuisine. Bring the family for cool games for the kids and shop the crafts on display. Festival proceeds benefit children's charities and programs sponsored by the Kiwanis Club of St. Martinville. It's the hottest little festival going!

337.394.9396 • www.pepperfestival.org

Hot Stuff

1 pound ground beef
½ onion, chopped
1 cup frozen sliced carrots
1 cup frozen cauliflower
3 to 4 stalks celery, chopped
1 can cream of mushroom soup
2 tablespoons soy sauce
½ teaspoon white pepper
1 (12-ounce) bag chow-mein noodles

Fry ground beef and onion, breaking up hamburger into small pieces. Drain and place in large baking dish. Combine vegetables, soup, soy sauce and pepper; stir into meat. Add ⅔ chow-mein noodles, mix and cover. Bake 30 to 40 minutes at 350°. Sprinkle remaining noodles on top. Bake uncovered another 10 to 15 minutes.

S. Thompson, New Orleans

State Capitol Building, Baton Rouge © Patric Steib

State Capitol Building
Baton Rouge

Cajun Chow Mein

1 pound ground beef,
  browned (preferably chuck)
½ (16-ounce) bag frozen Creole Seasoning Vegetable Mix
  (or 1 chopped onion, 1 chopped bell pepper and 1 cup chopped celery)
1 can onion soup
1 can cream of mushroom soup
2 cans Chinese vegetables chop suey
1 tablespoon soy sauce
1½ cups long grain rice (hot or mild)
1 teaspoon salt
1 teaspoon black pepper
1 teaspoon garlic powder

Mix all ingredients together (do not drain liquids). Put in a large greased casserole dish with top. Bake at 350° for 1 hour. If rice is not soft, cook another 20 to 30 minutes.

Ms. Ellie Zernott & the Louisiana Beef Industry Council

Bayou Meatloaf

1 tablespoon sea salt
1 teaspoon cayenne pepper
1 teaspoon black pepper
½ teaspoon cumin powder
4 tablespoons butter
1 cup finely chopped celery
1 bell pepper, finely chopped
1 small onion, minced
¼ cup chopped greens onions
½ teaspoon minced garlic
1 tablespoon hot sauce
1 tablespoon Worcestershire sauce
2 pounds ground beef
2 pound ground pork
3 eggs, beaten
1 cup very fine dry breadcrumbs (or more)
½ cup ketchup
½ cup milk

In a skillet combine the first 12 ingredients and brown. Add to a large bowl with ground meat, eggs and bread crumbs. Mix well adding in milk and ketchup. Add more breadcrumbs as needed. Form into 2 loaves and place in a deep-sided baking pan. Bake uncovered at 350° for 45 minutes. If desired, coat with a layer of ketchup covered with shredded cheese the last 10 minutes of cook time.

Louisiana Stuffed Meatloaf

2 cups herb-seasoned stuffing mix,
    crushed (divided)
1 carrot, shredded
1 cup salad shrimp, thawed
2 tablespoons parsley
¼ cup water
2 pounds ground beef
2 cans cream of mushroom soup, divided
1 egg, beaten
⅓ cup finely chopped onion (optional)
1 teaspoon salt
¼ cup milk

In a bowl, combine 1 cup stuffing mix, carrot, shrimp, parsley and water. Mix well and set aside. In another bowl, combine beef, 1 can soup, egg, onion, salt and remaining 1 cup stuffing mix. Shape into a two equal loaf portions. Place one portion in a greased baking dish and make an indention down the middle leaving a 1-inch margin around edges. Spread stuffing mixture inside indention. Place second loaf on top and pinch edges together. Bake at 350° about 35 to 45 minutes or until done. Cover with foil if needed. With 10 minutes of bake time remaining, combine 1 can soup with milk and spread evenly over loaf; return to oven to complete baking.

Bayou Burgers with Creole Mayo

Bayou Burgers:

1 pound ground chuck
½ pound hot ground sausage
½ cup chopped onion
½ cup skim milk
1 egg, beaten
½ teaspoon dry mustard
½ teaspoon salt
2 tablespoons Creole seasoning

Creole Mayo:

½ cup mayonnaise
½ tablespoon hot sauce
Parsley
Black pepper to taste
Dash Worcestershire sauce

Combine all Bayou Burgers ingredients; mix well. Shape burgers and grill to desired doneness. Combine Creole Mayo ingredients in a bowl and chill. Top burgers with Creole Mayo and other toppings. Serve on French bread slices.

Andouille Burgers

1½ pounds ground beef
1 pound ground andouille sausage
1 egg, beaten
½ cup minced onion
½ cup minced mushrooms
Salt, pepper and garlic powder

Mix all ingredients together and form into burgers. Cook on grill, or pan bake until done. Serve on French rolls with favorite toppings

Bayou Beef Italian

1 pound ground beef
1 pound chopped Italian sausage
1 onion, chopped
1 green bell pepper, chopped
1 tablespoon garlic, minced
2 cans diced tomatoes
1 can tomato soup
Salt and pepper
1 teaspoon oregano
1 teaspoon hot sauce (or more)
½ tablespoon butter
2 cups macaroni, uncooked

Sometimes I make this with rice. It just depends on my mood. I also switch out using Italian sausage and andouille sausage. Both make for a great dish.

Brown beef, sausage, onion, bell pepper, and garlic; drain. Add to crockpot along with 1½ cups water, tomatoes and soup. Stir in salt, pepper, oregano, hot sauce and butter. Mix well and cook on low 6 hours. Stir in uncooked macaroni and cook 2 to 3 hours more.

Ben & Linda Campbell, LSU Football Fans

Cajun Stuffed Eggplant

3 medium eggplants,
　split in half lengthwise
4 to 6 slices bacon
1 onion, chopped
1 green bell pepper, chopped
½ cup chopped celery
2 cloves garlic, minced
½ pound ground pork
½ pound ground beef
1 can diced tomatoes
1 teaspoon hot sauce
½ teaspoon thyme
½ teaspoon oregano
½ teaspoon salt
½ cup dry breadcrumbs
¾ cup grated Parmesan cheese, divided

Place eggplant halves in large pot of boiling salted water; boil 20 to 30 minutes or until tender. Remove from water and scoop out pulp without breaking skin. Reserve hollowed out shells; set pulp and shells aside. Preheat oven to 350°. In a large skillet, cook bacon until crisp; drain. When cooled, crumble bacon and set aside. In the same skillet, cook onion, bell pepper, celery and garlic until tender. Add pork and beef; cook until meat is browned. Drain fat. Stir in reserved eggplant pulp, breaking into small pieces. Add reserved bacon, tomatoes, hot sauce, thyme, oregano and salt; simmer 5 minutes. Remove from heat. Stir in breadcrumbs and ½ cup cheese. Spoon mixture into shells. Top with remaining cheese. Bake 20 to 30 minutes at 350°.

Renee Hebert & Family

Louisiana Meat Pies

Crust:

4¼ cups flour, divided
2 teaspoons salt
½ cup melted shortening
2 eggs
1 cup milk
Salt, black and cayenne pepper to taste

Cut shortening into flour and salt; add eggs and milk. Shape into a ball and refrigerate 2 hours. With about 30 minutes of refrigeration time left, prepare Filling. Roll out dough and cut round shapes. Place some meat mixture in each circle, then flip half over to form a half circle. Seal edges together with a fork. Prick holes on top with fork. Fry in hot oil or bake at 350° until golden brown.

Filling:

1 pound ground pork
1 pound ground beef
1 cup chopped green onions
1 bell pepper, chopped
¼ cup chopped parsley
2 tablespoons Worcestershire sauce
1 tablespoon lemon juice
Pinch ground cloves
¼ cup flour

Brown meats. Add onions, bell pepper and parsley; cook 5 minutes. Remove from heat. Add Worcestershire, lemon juice and cloves; mix well. Add flour and mix. Add a little water, if mixture is dry.

Kyle LaBlanc www.crawdads.net

Andouille & Chicken Cajun Meat Pie

3 tablespoons flour
3 tablespoons oil
1 pound ground andouille sausage
1 pound ground chicken or turkey
1 sweet onion, minced
1 tablespoon hot sauce
2 cans green chiles
Salt, pepper and garlic powder to taste
2 large frozen pie crusts, thawed
Butter, melted

Brown flour and oil together to make a roux. Remove from heat and set aside. In a large skillet, brown meats; drain. Add onions, hot sauce and chiles; stir. Stir in roux; add salt, pepper and garlic powder to taste. Remove crusts from foil pan to release suction; return crusts to their pan a bit off center. Place equal portions of meat mixture to one side of each pie crust. Fold crust over and pinch edges. Center pie in pan, brush with butter and bake at 350° until golden.

Traditionally, Red Beans & Rice was served on Monday, because that was wash day.

Bobbi Lynne's "Cheaters" Red Beans & Rice

1 box Tony Chachere's or Zatarain's
   Red Beans & Rice box mix
1 (14-ounce) can dark red kidney beans,
   drained
⅔ cup quick barley, uncooked
½ pound lean smoked turkey sausage,
   sliced into ½-inch pieces
Olive oil
½ bell pepper, diced
½ white or yellow onion, minced
½ tablespoon garlic infused olive oil
½ teaspoon black pepper
1 teaspoon Cajun seasoning

For Cajun seasoning, Bobbi Lynne recommends Fontenot and a Half Cajun Seasoning which is available by calling 225.749.4049 or at www.fontenotandahalf.com.

In a large pot, combine box mix with water as called for on box directions. Add kidney beans, barley and sausage. Cook over medium-high heat until it comes to a boil. While waiting, heat olive to cover bottom of a large frying pan. Sauté peppers and onions, seasoning them with the pepper and Cajun seasoning. Cook until onions are somewhat translucent. Once main pot has reached a boil, add sautéed vegetables. Cover, reduce heat to medium, and simmer, stirring frequently, approximately 20 minutes or until rice and barley are fully cooked. Remove from heat and let rest 10 to 15 minutes so sauce can thicken.

Bobbi Lynne Shackelford, Lafayette

Ham Red Beans and Rice

3 cups red kidney beans
6 cups water
½ pound cubed ham
1 large onion, chopped
1 green bell pepper, chopped
2 cloves garlic, minced
1 bay leaf
½ teaspoon salt
½ teaspoon pepper
1 tablespoon flour
2 tablespoons hot sauce

Wash beans well; put in covered pot with 6 cups water. Add ham and slowly bring to boil. Add onions, bell pepper, garlic, bay leaf, salt and pepper. Simmer 2 hours, stirring occasionally, until beans are soft. Stir in flour and hot sauce. Serve over rice.

LOUISIANA SWINE FESTIVAL

First Full Weekend in November ◆ Basile

Our festival is held annually the first full weekend in November. Visitors enjoy our hog calling, boudin eating and pig chase contests, carnival, pork cook-off, exciting line up of music, food and our parade.

337.432.6807 ◆ www.laswinefestival.com

Red Beans and Rice

1 pound red beans,
   soaked overnight in twice as much water
1 pound smoked sausage, sliced cross-sectionally
1 pound ham, medium diced (or 2 to 3 ham hocks or tasso)
8 ounces (1 cup) onions, medium dice
4 ounces (½ cup) celery, medium dice
4 ounces (½ cup) bell pepper, medium dice
3 tablespoons minced garlic
½ cup white wine
1 teaspoon each dried basil, oregano, thyme
2 bay leaves
Salt, pepper, cayenne to taste

Drain soaked beans, rinse thoroughly under cold water, and start cooking them in a large Dutch oven with enough water to cover them 2 inches over the top bean layer.   Add 1 tablespoon salt. Pan broil sausage and ham and add to the beans when browned thoroughly. Sweat the mire poix (vegetables) in the sausage grease, add garlic and cook 1 minute longer. Deglaze pan with wine, add herbs and reduce slightly. Add to beans and simmer until tender, about 1½ to 2 hours. Serve over hot, long-grain rice with cornbread, greens and/or a green salad. Serves 10 to 12.

Chef Ross Headlee, Louisiana Culinary Institute

Sherrie's Bedtime Bar-B-Que Pork

Pork Roast
1 can Pepsi
1 large onion, chopped
1 small jar minced garlic
1 bottle barbecue sauce

This pork barbecue is perfect for making overnight.

Just before going to bed, put pork roast, Pepsi, onion and garlic in crockpot; cook on low. When you awaken, the pork will shred very easily. Shred pork, add barbecue sauce and simmer about 15 minutes. All done!

Sherrie Henne, Now a New York Cajun

OLDIES BUT GOODIES FEST & SMOKIN' OLDIES BBQ COOK-OFF

2nd weekend in October • Port Allen

This State Championship BBQ Contest starts on Saturday each year with live music at 2:00 pm. On Sunday, there is a poker run, antique car show, hula hoop, jitterbug, twist contest and children's activities. Live bands featuring 50's, 60's & 70's music start at noon. All proceeds go to Dream Day Foundation/St. Judes Children's Hospital. Hours are from 11:00 am - 6:00 pm.

225.344.2920 • www.westbatonrouge.net

Chef Ross' Pulled Pork

1 cup kosher salt
½ cup brown sugar
¼ cup cracked black pepper
1 teaspoon mustard powder
1 tablespoon garlic powder
1 tablespoon chili powder
1 teaspoon cumin
1 teaspoon allspice
1 cup Worcestershire sauce
1 ounce liquid smoke
1 (5- to 8-pound) Boston butt pork roast,
   excess outer fat removed

Combine all ingredients, except pork roast. Season roast and smoke in a smoke barbeque pit about 3 hours. Remove and cover with aluminum foil, and finish in a 350° oven for 2 hours or until roast reaches an internal temperature of 200°. Remove from oven, take out the bone (it will separate easily from the meat) and shred meat with a fork. Serve on a large platter with a mustard-based barbeque sauce with white bread, coleslaw, potato salad and beans.

Chef Ross Headlee, Louisiana Culinary Institute

Mustard Ham

1 (12- to 14-pound) ham, bone-in
Whole cloves
1 (16-ounce) package light brown sugar
1 cup yellow mustard
1 (8-ounce) jar maraschino cherries, drained
12 ounces ginger ale
1 can pineapple rings

Heat oven to 325°. Stud ham with cloves. Place ham in baking pan, cover with foil and bake per directions on package. With 1 hour cook time remaining, combine brown sugar and mustard; add ginger ale and mix well. Remove ham from oven and baste with sauce. Cover and return to oven. With 30 minutes cook time remaining, remove ham again. Arrange pineapple rings and cherries on ham, securing with toothpicks. Baste and cook an additional 30 minutes.

Smoked Cajun Pork Barbecue

1 pork butt
½ cup each ketchup and mustard
½ cup each hot sauce and vinegar
½ cup Salt, pepper, cumin powder and garlic powder to taste

Rinse pork butt and place in a covered dish. Combine remaining ingredients and pour over pork butt. Marinate in refrigerator overnight. Prepare covered smoker or grill for indirect cooking with charcoal and hickory or mesquite. Place meat over hottest and cook for an hour, turning and basting often (edges should be brown). Move to coolest part and smoke covered several hours. Keep a temperature of around 300° and keep lid closed as long as possible. After removing from smoker, allow to rest about 10 minutes. Pull or chop and serve hot with your favorite sauce on French bread.

Rolled & Stuffed Pork Chops

6 thin boneless pork chops
2 to 3 cloves garlic, minced
1 stick butter, softened
Salt and pepper
6 slices pepper jack cheese
1 onion, finely diced
½ green bell pepper, finely diced
1 small can chopped black olives
1 (16-ounce) can chicken broth

Pork chops can be pounded thinner, if desired. Rub each pork chop with garlic and butter; sprinkle with salt and pepper to taste. Place 1 slice pepper jack cheese on each chop then top with onions, bell peppers, and black olives. (It won't take much to fill each chop; reserve left-over vegetables.)   Fold over each chop and secure with a toothpick. Place stuffed and rolled chops in a covered dish. Add chicken broth and any remaining vegetables. Cover and cook at 350° degrees until pork is done. Serve hot over rice.

Andouille Rigatoni Bake

1 tablespoon cooking oil
1 pound andouille sausage, 1-inch pieces
1 onion, chopped
2 ribs celery, chopped
1 green bell pepper, chopped
1 red bell pepper, chopped
2 cloves garlic, minced
2 cans crushed tomatoes
1 teaspoon salt
½ teaspoon freshly-ground black pepper
¾ pound large rigatoni pasta
1 cup sour cream

In a large frying pan, heat oil over medium heat. Add sausage and cook, stirring, for 3 minutes. Stir in onion, celery, green and red bell pepper and garlic. Cover pan, lower heat to medium-low, and cook (stirring occasionally) until vegetables are soft, about 10 minutes. Add tomatoes, salt and black pepper. Cover and simmer 15 minutes longer.   In a large pot of boiling, salted water, cook rigatoni until just done, about 14 minutes. Drain and toss pasta with sauce. Combine all in a casserole dish and stir in sour cream. Bake at 400° about 15 to 20 minutes. Serve hot.

S. Thompson, New Orleans

Mom's Chicken & Sausage Linguine Casserole

3 cloves crushed garlic
½ cup chopped onion
½ cup chopped celery
1 pound boneless chicken, cubed
2 to 3 tablespoons butter
½ pound ground hot sausage
1 pound linguine
1 (16-ounce) can tomato sauce
¼ cup hot water
4 ounces sliced, drained mushrooms
Salt and pepper to taste
1 tablespoon Italian seasoning
Dash hot sauce
4 ounces Mozzarella cheese

Brown garlic, onion, celery and chicken in butter. Add sausage and cook until done; drain. Cook linguine as per box directions; drain. Mix tomato sauce, hot water and mushrooms in a bowl. Salt and pepper to taste; add Italian seasoning. Combine all in a casserole dish and bake at 325° for 20 to 25 minutes. My mom used to layer this casserole. Sometimes I do, but most often I just stir it all up and bake it. Either way it is wonderful.

Darnel & Beckia Johnston, GO LSU TIGERS

Cajun Chicken & Dumplings

4 boneless skinless chicken thighs,
 cut in small chunks
1 can cream of chicken soup
1 can cream of mushroom soup
2 cups water
¼ cup chopped onion
¼ cup chopped bell pepper
¼ cup chopped celery
¼ cup white wine
2 chicken bouillon cubes
Salt and pepper to taste
1 tablespoon hot sauce
1 small package refrigerated biscuits

Combine all ingredients, except biscuits, in pot and stir to mix. Cover and cook on low 2 hours. Increase heat slightly. Tear biscuits in half and add to crockpot. Stir gently to submerge biscuits. Cook on high 30 to 40 minutes.

© Rick Lord • bigstockphoto.com

Louisiana

Chicken Etouffée

2 chicken breasts
Olive oil
1 small onion, finely chopped
1 bell pepper, finely chopped
½ cup minced celery
2 tablespoons chopped green onions
½ tablespoon minced garlic
½ tablespoon Cajun seasoning
½ stick butter
⅔ cup flour
⅔ cup oil
2 cans chicken broth

Chop chicken into bite-size pieces; add to cast-iron skillet with a small bit of olive oil and cook over medium heat until done. Add onions and bell pepper and cook until vegetables are soft. Add celery, green onions, garlic, Cajun seasoning and butter. While chicken and vegetables are cooking, make a roux using ⅔ cup flour and ⅔ cup oil; cook over low heat until brown. Add roux to cast-iron skillet and mix well. Add chicken broth and cook about 30 minutes over medium heat. Serve hot with rice and French bread.

Charlie's Chicken Jambalaya

¼ cup vegetable oil
2 onions, chopped
6 green onions, chopped
2 medium green bell peppers, chopped
1 broiler-fryer chicken, cut into 8 pieces
½ pound ham, cubed
½ pound smoked sausage, cut into ½-inch slices
2 cans diced tomatoes
1 can tomato paste
1 teaspoon salt
1¾ cups uncooked rice
1 cup water
1 tablespoon hot sauce

In large pot or Dutch oven, heat oil. Add onions, green onions and peppers; cook 10 minutes or until tender. Add chicken and brown on all sides, about 10 minutes. Add ham, sausage, tomatoes, tomato paste and salt. Cover and simmer 10 minutes; stir in rice. Add water. Cover and simmer 1 hour or until chicken is done stirring frequently. Add additional water if rice begins to stick to bottom of pan. Before serving, stir in hot sauce.

Charlie Tucker

Chicken & Black-Eyed Peas

1 tablespoon salt
2½ teaspoons onion powder
4½ teaspoons garlic powder
1 teaspoon white pepper
1 teaspoon dry mustard
2½ teaspoons rubbed sage, divided
1½ teaspoons dried thyme leaves, divided
1½ pounds chicken, cubed
1 cup flour
Vegetable oil
¼ cup chicken fat, pork lard or shortening
9 slices bacon, ½-inch pieces
3 medium onions, finely chopped
1½ cups finely chopped celery
3 bay leaves
2 tablespoons hot sauce, divided
1 pound dried black-eyed peas
11 cups chicken stock or water

In a small bowl, combine salt, 1½ teaspoons onion powder, 3½ teaspoons garlic powder, white pepper, dry mustard, 1 teaspoon sage and ½ teaspoon thyme; mix well. Sprinkle 1 tablespoon on chicken pieces; pat in with hand. Combine remaining mixture with flour in a plastic bag; set aside. In large skillet, over medium-high heat, bring ½ inch oil to 350°. Dredge chicken in seasoned flour. Fry in oil. In large saucepan or Dutch oven melt fat over medium-high heat. Add bacon, cook 3 to 4 minutes or just until it starts to crisp. Stir in onions, celery, bay leaves and 1 tablespoon hot sauce. Cook 5 minutes, stirring frequently. Stir in black-eyed peas, remaining 1 teaspoon garlic powder, 1 teaspoon onion powder, 1½ teaspoons sage, and 1 teaspoon thyme. Cook 2 to 4 minutes or until liquid is absorbed; stir frequently. Add stock, chicken pieces and remaining 1 tablespoon hot sauce. Simmer covered and cook about 2 hours or until peas are tender; stir occasionally. Remove bay leaves. Serve with rice.

Beau "Lil Bo" Joshland

Good Ole Fried Chicken

1 fryer chicken, cut-up
¾ cup all-purpose flour
3 teaspoons seasoned salt
1 teaspoon garlic powder
½ teaspoon onion powder
¾ teaspoon pepper
¼ teaspoon chili powder
¼ cup bacon drippings or vegetable shortening

Clean and rinse chicken; pat dry and set aside. In a brown paper or plastic bag, add flour and seasoning; shake well. Place chicken in bag, 1 piece at a time, and shake to coat. Shake excess flour from each piece and place it on a plate. Repeat process until you run out of mix. Melt bacon drippings and enough shortening to make 1 inch of cooking oil in a skillet. Heat over medium heat. When oil is hot, add chicken and fry until golden brown and chicken juices run clear. Turn as needed.

Battered Festival Chicken

8 skinless, boneless chicken breasts
Hot sauce
Salt and pepper
2 cups buttermilk, divided
1 egg, beaten
2 to 3 cups self-rising flour
1 can Rotel
Oil for frying
Flour for dredging

This recipe works with whole boneless breasts, chicken tenders and large cubed chicken. I have even used it with fish, gator, stew meat and such.

Marinate chicken in desired amount of hot sauce, salt, pepper and ¼ cup buttermilk. Cover and chill overnight. In a bowl, combine remaining buttermilk, egg, flour and Rotel. Mix into a thick batter. Heat oil. Dredge each piece of chicken in flour and dip in batter. Fry in hot oil until golden and chicken is done. Serve hot.

Beau "Lil Bo" Joshland

Crockpot Mushroom Chicken

6 skinless bone-in breast halves
1½ teaspoons salt
¼ teaspoon pepper
½ teaspoon paprika
¼ teaspoon lemon pepper
1 teaspoon garlic powder
1 (10¾-ounce) cream of mushroom soup
8 ounces sour cream
½ can chicken broth
½ pound fresh mushrooms

Rinse chicken and pat dry. Combine salt, pepper, paprika, lemon pepper, garlic powder. Rub over chicken and place in crockpot. Combine soup, sour cream and broth. Pour over chicken. Cover and cook on low 6 to 8 hours. Serve over potatoes or rice.

John Ebert

St. Louis Cathedral
Historic Jackson Square
New Orleans

Creole Tomato Chicken Breasts

2 tablespoons butter
2 chicken breasts
Salt and pepper to taste
1 cup finely chopped onion
1 cup finely chopped celery
1 cup finely chopped bell peppers
2 tablespoons finely minced garlic
2 tablespoon flour
1 can chopped tomatoes
1 bay leaf
2 tablespoons parsley
1 tablespoon paprika

Melt butter in a black cast iron skillet. Sprinkle chicken on both sides with salt and pepper and brown evenly. Remove to a plate. Add onion, celery, bell peppers and garlic to skillet and cook until onion is golden. Add remaining ingredients and stir well. Return reserved chicken to skillet and cook until warm and cooked through. Serve chicken covered in sauce.

Hot Sauced Sticky Chicken

1 onion, chopped
1 bell pepper chopped
2 tablespoons minced garlic
1 teaspoon cayenne pepper
1 tablespoon hot sauce
Butter
4 to 6 chicken boneless breasts, cubed
Cajun seasoning
1 can pineapple chunks, undrained
½ cup hot sauce
⅔ cups honey
¼ cup sesame seeds

In a small skillet, add onions, bell peppers, garlic and cayenne pepper with enough butter for sautéing. Cook 5 minutes over medium heat. Place chicken in a large glass baking dish, with lid, and sprinkle with Cajun seasoning. Cover with cooked vegetables. Top with hot sauce, honey and pineapple with juice. Sprinkle sesame seeds over top. Bake covered at 350° for 35 minutes. Bake uncovered until top is browned.

Cajun Baked Chicken Thighs

6 to 10 chicken thighs
2 chicken bouillon cubes
1 cup boiling water
4 teaspoons Worcestershire sauce
2 cloves garlic, minced
2 teaspoons curry powder
2 teaspoons dried oregano leaves
1 teaspoon salt
1 teaspoon dry mustard
1 teaspoon paprika
½ teaspoon hot sauce

Place chicken in a large shallow baking pan. Dissolve bouillon cubes in water; add to pan. Add Worcestershire sauce, garlic, curry, oregano, salt, mustard, paprika and hot sauce; mix well. Spoon mixture over chicken and bake at 375° for 20 minutes. Turn chicken and baste with pan juices. Continue baking 15 to 30 minutes or until chicken is done. Serve hot.

Easy Cajun Honey Mustard Chicken

8 to 10 chicken leg quarters
1 cup honey mustard
½ cup barbecue sauce
½ cup hot sauce

Rinse chicken. Combine sauce ingredients. Add chicken to sauce and refrigerate overnight (or at least several hours). Grill over medium high heat, basting with remaining sauce. Do not baste during last 5 minutes to allow heat to cook chicken juices in marinade. Turn as needed. Cook until juices run clear. Serve hot. You can also bake this recipe in a 350° oven. Serve hot with choice of sides.

Tiger Tater Casserole

1 (24-ounce) bag hash browns,
   thawed
1 pound smoked sausage, chopped
½ pound cooked chicken, small cubed
1 tablespoon cayenne pepper
2 cans cream of chicken soup
2 cups sour cream
1 cup grated pepper jack cheese
1½ sticks butter, divided
⅓ cup chopped onion
Salt and pepper to taste
2 cups crushed cornflakes

This is our favorite LSU game day recipe—a real "stick to your bones" meal. Make it ahead of time in a foil pan and chill. Then reheat it on the grill's upper rack. Delicious made and served at home, too.

In a large mixing bowl, combine hash browns, sausage, chicken, cayenne pepper, soup, sour cream, cheese, 1 stick melted butter, onion and salt and pepper to taste. (Do not brown smoked sausage because juices help season the recipe.) Mix well. Spoon into a large baking pan. Melt another ½ stick butter, combine with cornflakes, and sprinkle over top. Bake at 350° for 30 minutes.

Darnel & Beckia Johnston, Go LSU Tigers

Cajun Fried Turkey

10 gallons peanut oil
1 (10- to 15-pound) turkey
6 teaspoons salt
6 teaspoons paprika
6 teaspoons white pepper
6 teaspoons cayenne
6 teaspoons accent, optional
16 ounces liquid crab boil concentrate

Do not cook this indoors. Rinse turkey inside and out and remove neck and packing pieces. Combine remaining ingredients and inject turkey every 1 to 2 inches. Cover turkey with cling wrap and refrigerate overnight. Follow directions for your fryer on measuring oil amounts and set-up. Heat oil to 350° (outdoors) in fryer. Put turkey in basket and CAREFULLY lower it into pot. Cook 5 minutes per pound. Check in 1 hour using a meat thermometer. Cut-off heat source before removing from fryer. Allow to rest 5 minutes before slicing.

Creole-Smoked Turkey Lasagna

Butter for frying
½ cup chopped onions
8 ounces fresh sliced mushrooms
3 cloves garlic, minced
2 tablespoons Creole seasoning
1 pound cooked smoked turkey, small cubed
3 cups tomato sauce
2 teaspoons basil
½ teaspoon oregano
Pepper to taste
1 (8-ounce) package oven-ready lasagna noodles
2 cups cottage cheese
8 ounces grated mozzarella cheese

Melt butter in a skillet over medium-high heat; brown onions, mushrooms and garlic. Add turkey and Creole seasoning. Add tomato sauce, basil, oregano and pepper; reduce heat. Lay ⅓ noodles on bottom of 9x13-inch pan. Add ½ cottage cheese, ⅓ tomato sauce and ⅓ cheese. Repeat layers, finish with remaining noodles, remaining sauce and remaining cheese. Cover with aluminum foil and bake 35 to 40 minutes at 350°.

Grilled Game Hens

4 game hens
1 teaspoon salt
1 teaspoon cayenne pepper
1 teaspoon paprika
½ teaspoon white pepper
½ teaspoon black pepper
½ teaspoon oregano
¼ teaspoon garlic powder
¼ teaspoon onion powder
½ cup lemon juice
¼ cup vegetable oil

Rinse hens and set aside. Combine remaining ingredients in a large bowl. Evenly coat each hen in mixture and store, chilled, overnight in a zip-closed bag or covered dish. Place hens on hot grill over medium heat on a covered grill. Cook to brown edges and give grill marks. Spray with nonstick spray and wrap in foil. Cook on grill over medium heat for an additional 10 minutes to seal in juices. Leave lightly wrapped in foil when serving.

Mushroom Duck Breasts

4 duck breasts
Creole seasoning
Lemon juice
Flour
Olive oil
1 cup chopped celery
1 cup chopped onion
1 cup sliced mushrooms
Red wine
Salt and pepper to taste
2 teaspoons thyme
2 teaspoons garlic powder
½ cup real bacon bits

Rinse duck breasts. Sprinkle evenly with Creole seasoning and lemon juice. Dredge each breast in flour and brown in an iron skillet with olive oil over medium heat. Stir in onions, celery and mushrooms. Add a few spoonfuls of red wine. Add salt, pepper, thyme and garlic powder. Serve duck covered with vegetables and juice and sprinkled with bacon bits.

BRUDLEY'S WILD GAME, SEAFOOD & JAMBALAYA COOK-OFF

November • New Iberia

Brudley's Wild Game, Seafood & Jambalaya Cook-Off is a fundraising event for the Iberia Boys and Girls Club. The event features around 25 teams competing in various categories. The $20 admission ($10 children) benefits the Boys and Girls Club and is your all you can eat ticket to some great dishes. In addition to delicious food, you will be entertained by live music from two bands -- one zydeco and one pop-country band. Join us for the fun, family friendly event.

337.268.9555 x100 • www.bgcacadiana.com

Cajun Rabbit

2½ pounds rabbit meat,
  boned
½ cup olive or vegetable oil
1 medium onion, sliced
½ cup all-purpose flour
Salt and pepper
1 cup chicken broth
2 cups sliced mushrooms
½ cup chicken broth
1 tablespoon hot sauce
½ tablespoon minced garlic
1 cup chopped celery
1 can chopped tomatoes, drained
1 can small pitted ripe olives, drained

Rinse meat and set aside. Heat oil in large covered skillet. Cook onion in oil, stirring frequently, until tender. Reduce heat to medium. Coat rabbit with flour and ½ teaspoon each salt and pepper. Cook rabbit in skillet with onions, turning occasionally, until brown. Sprinkle with more salt and pepper. Stir in chicken broth then remaining ingredients; mix well. Cover and simmer about 1 hour or until rabbit is tender.

IOWA RABBIT FESTIVAL

3rd week in March • Iowa

The Iowa Rabbit Festival is one of the top 20 festivals in the Southeastern United States, attracting over 20,000 people each year. You will enjoy live music, arts and craft booths, lots of great food, a huge carnival, pageant, and parade. The State Rabbit Show is a fun event with 400 Rabbits competing. All proceeds are donated back to our community. Hop on over to the Iowa Rabbit Festival where I guarantee you will have a Hare raising good time!

337.433.8475 • www.iowarabbitfestival.org

Fried Frog Legs

16 to 20 frog legs
3 cups buttermilk
½ teaspoon garlic juice
½ cup flour
½ cup cornmeal
½ tablespoon garlic powder
1 teaspoon paprika
½ teaspoon onion powder
½ teaspoon ground cayenne pepper
¼ teaspoon black pepper
1 dash each white pepper, oregano and rosemary
Salt to taste
Oil for frying

Skin, clean and rinse frog legs well. Cover with buttermilk and garlic juice in a bowl, cover and refrigerate overnight. Heat oil in skillet. Combine flour, cornmeal and spices; mix well. Dredge frog legs evenly in breading. Heat oil in a skillet and fry until golden brown.

Buffalo Frog Legs

2 dozen frog legs
1 package fish batter mix plus ingredients to prepare per directions
½ cup hot sauce
1 stick butter, melted
Ranch dressing

Rinse frog legs. Prepare fish batter as directed on package. Dip legs in batter and fry in a deep fryer with hot oil until golden brown. Combine hot sauce and butter. Toss legs in sauce mix to coat evenly. Serve with ranch dressing for dipping.

Frog Legs and Mushrooms Teriyaki

¼ cup margarine
2 cups chopped onions
1 cup chopped bell pepper
1 cup snipped fresh parsley
1 pound mushrooms, sliced
2 tablespoons minced garlic
1½ teaspoons salt
3 tablespoons hot sauce
2 cups deboned frog leg meat
½ cup dry white wine
½ cup teriyaki sauce

In a large wok or pot, melt margarine. Add onions, bell pepper and parsley. Sauté until onions are clear. Add mushrooms and garlic. Stir well and continue to cook until mushrooms are hot. Add salt, hot sauce and frog leg meat; stir well. Add wine and teriyaki sauce. Reduce heat to medium-low and simmer 10 minutes. May be served over rice.

Chef Lauren Aswell & Seafood Promotion and Marketing Board

Sweet & Sour Alligator

2 eggs, beaten
¼ cup plus 2 tablespoons all-purpose flour, divided
2 tablespoons milk
1 teaspoon salt
1½ pounds alligator tail meat, cubed
4 cups vegetable oil
1 cup pineapple juice
⅓ cup firmly packed brown sugar
3 tablespoons cornstarch
1 (8-ounce) can tomato sauce
⅓ cup cider vinegar
⅓ cup light corn syrup
½ teaspoon garlic salt
¼ teaspoon black pepper
1 (8-ounce) can unsweetened pineapple chunks
1 medium bell pepper, chopped
2 stalks celery, chopped
½ medium onion, chopped

Combine eggs, flour, milk and salt; mix well. Add alligator cubes, stirring to coat. In 2-quart deep fryer, heat oil to 350°. Deep-fry alligator a few pieces at a time until golden brown. Drain well. In a 4-quart saucepan, combine pineapple juice, brown sugar, cornstarch, tomato sauce, vinegar, corn syrup, garlic salt and pepper. Stir well. Cook over medium heat, stirring constantly, until thickened. Stir in alligator chunks, pineapple, bell pepper, celery and onion. Cover and simmer 10 minutes. Serve over hot rice.

Chef Kirk Tucker & Seafood Promotion and Marketing Board

Hot Gator

1 pound gator meat,
   small cubed
Hot sauce
Soy sauce
Garlic powder
Salt and pepper
Flour for dredging
Hot oil

Marinate gator meat in hot sauce and soy sauce to taste. Sprinkle with garlic powder, salt and pepper to taste. Poke each piece with a fork to soften and allow marinade to sink in. Chill, covered, 1 hour. Dredge each piece in flour and pan fry in oil until golden. Serve hot with rice.

Seared Gator Strips with Red Sauce

1 pound gator meat, cut into chicken strip sizes
3 tablespoons butter
1 cup minced onions
1 green bell pepper, chopped

1 garlic clove, minced
Salt and pepper to taste
½ cup red wine
Sour cream

Melt butter in skillet; add gator strips, onions, bell pepper, garlic, salt and pepper. Cook until meat is golden on the outside and white on the inside. Remove meat from skillet. Add red wine to pan and stir to mix with vegetables; reduce slightly. Remove from heat. Add sour cream, a spoonful a time, stirring well each time, until sauce reaches desired thickness. Serve strips over French bread covered in sauce.

Red Peppered Chitterlings

5 pounds frozen chitterlings, thawed
5 cups water
2 tablespoons red pepper flakes
2 stalks celery, with leaves
2 large onions, chopped
2 bay leaves
1 clove garlic, minced
½ cup vinegar
1 teaspoon salt
½ teaspoon pepper
1 red pepper, cut in pieces (optional)

Soak chitterlings in cold water at least 3 hours. Drain, rinse and remove excess fat and dirt. Repeat rinse 2 times making sure they are completely clean of all material. Cut into small (1-inch) pieces. Place in full pot of water with all ingredients and cover. Cook over medium heat 3 hours. Serve with vinegar or hot sauce.

Stephen Nash, Baton Rouge

Fish & Seafood

Stuffed Flounder

Stuffing:

¾ stick butter
¼ cup chopped celery
¾ cup chopped onion
1 small clove garlic, minced
3 teaspoons green onion tops
3 teaspoons chopped bell pepper
¼ teaspoon each salt and pepper
1½ ounces white wine
1 pound white crabmeat
⅓ cup breadcrumbs

Melt butter in skillet. Sauté celery, onions, garlic, green onions and bell pepper. Salt and pepper to taste; add wine. Simmer 5 minutes. Add crabmeat and breadcrumbs. Mix well and place directly into flounder cavity.

Flounder:

1 ounce olive oil
1 (1-pound) flounder
2 lemons
Salt and pepper

Oil a baking dish large enough for flounder to spread out. Split flounder from behind gills to tail and lift skin and meat one side at a time while running filet knife along backbone until total backbone is exposed and completely removed. Place flounder in dish dark side up. Open sides of flounder and apply juice of 1 lemon to all meat. Salt and pepper. Top with Stuffing and pull sides of flounder over stuffing. Thin slice remaining lemon and place slices over entire fish. Lightly salt and pepper. Cover with foil and bake in 350° oven for 20 minutes. Remove foil and bake an additional 10 minutes. Serves 4.

Creole Red Snapper

1 tablespoon vegetable oil
3 tomatoes, peeled and coarsely chopped
1 large onion, chopped
1 green bell pepper, chopped
1 celery stalk, chopped
3 cloves garlic, minced
1½ cups water
¾ cup uncooked rice
1 teaspoon ground cumin
½ teaspoon dried thyme leaves
½ teaspoon hot sauce
1 bay leaf
1½ pounds red snapper filets with skin, cut into 2-inch pieces
¼ cup chopped parsley

This is one of my favorite dishes. You have to be careful when you make it so you don't break up the filets. And if you do, it still tastes good

In large skillet heat oil; add tomatoes, onion, bell pepper, celery and garlic. Cook 5 minutes. Add water, rice, cumin, thyme, hot sauce and bay leaf. Bring to a boil; reduce heat and simmer covered 10 minutes. Add fish filets evenly and sprinkle with parsley. Cover and simmer 5 to 8 minutes until fish flakes. Remove bay leaf and serve filets hot over rice. Drizzle rice with pan drippings.

Danny Franklin

Creole Filet Parmesan

1 pound fish filets
2 tablespoons lemon juice
Cayenne pepper
½ cup grated Parmesan cheese
4 tablespoons (½ stick) butter, softened
3 tablespoons mayonnaise
3 tablespoons finely chopped green onions
¼ teaspoon seasoned salt
½ teaspoon dried basil
¼ teaspoon black pepper
Dash (or two!) hot pepper sauce

Preheat oven to 350°. In buttered 9x13-inch baking dish, lay filets in single layer. Sprinkle with cayenne pepper. Brush top with lemon juice. In bowl combine cheese, butter, mayonnaise, onions and seasonings. Mix well with fork. Bake fish in preheated oven 10 to 20 minutes or until fish just starts to flake. Spread with cheese mixture and bake until golden brown, about 5 minutes. Baking time will depend on the thickness of the fish you use.

Jerk Fish

4 to 6 white fish filets
½ cup orange juice
¼ cup fresh lime juice
½ teaspoon cumin
½ teaspoon minced garlic
2 jalapeno peppers, seeded and chopped

Lay filets in a glass baking dish. Combine remaining ingredients in bowl; pour over fish and marinate 30 minutes. Bake at 375° for 20 minutes or until fish flakes.

Blackened Fish

4 to 6 fish filets
1 teaspoon garlic powder
1 teaspoon black pepper
1 teaspoon white pepper
1 teaspoon thyme
1 teaspoon red pepper
1 teaspoon paprika
1 teaspoon salt
1 teaspoon onion powder
Melted butter

Lay fish in a shallow pan. Combine dry ingredients in a bowl. Brush each filet with melted butter and sprinkle evenly with seasoning mix. Bake uncovered at 400° until fish flakes (or pan cook in butter). Serve hot.

Broiled Horseradish Flounder

⅓ cup mayonnaise
4 tablespoons horseradish
4 flounder filets
¼ cup fresh lemon juice
Dash each cayenne pepper, garlic powder, salt and pepper

Combine mayonnaise and horseradish; set aside. Place flounder in a baking pan. Squeeze lemon juice over flounder. Sprinkle with seasonings. Allow to rest 5 minutes to soak in juice. Place under broiler for 5 minutes. Remove from oven and spread mayonnaise mixture on filets. Place under broiler and broil 5 more minutes until fish is flaky and topping is bubbly and golden brown.

Grilled Fish Orleans

2 tablespoons olive oil
6 medium-sized Louisiana shrimp
¼ cup brandy
4 cloves garlic
1 tablespoon chopped red pepper
2 tablespoons chopped green onion
¼ cup sliced mushrooms
¼ cup chopped artichoke hearts
¾ cup white wine
¼ cup butter
2 (6- to 8-ounce) Louisiana fish filets*
6 ounces pasta, cooked al dente
Fresh chopped parsley for garnish (optional)

Heat oil in sauté pan. Add shrimp and cook 2 to 3 minutes. Pour brandy over shrimp and ignite. Cover immediately to extinguish flame. Add garlic, red pepper, green onion, mushrooms and artichokes. Add white wine. Reduce heat. Add butter and blend slowly. Grill or pan-fry fish in separate pan. Place fish over pasta. Top with shrimp sauce. Garnish with fresh chopped parsley.

Note: *May use speckled trout, flounder, black drum, or grouper. May substitute Gulf of Mexico steaks of tuna, swordfish, shark, mackerel, or amberjack.

Seafood Promotion and Marketing Board, New Orleans

Mom's Fried Hot Catfish

2 pounds catfish filets
⅔ cup lemon juice
2 tablespoons hot sauce
⅔ cup flour
⅔ cup yellow cornmeal
Salt and pepper to taste
Vegetable oil for frying

Rinse catfish and set on paper towels. In shallow dish combine lemon juice and hot sauce; add fish. Cover and refrigerate 1 hour. When removing from refrigerator, turn fish to coat evenly. On a shallow plate, combine flour, cornmeal, salt and pepper. Coat fish with flour mixture and fry in hot oil until golden brown on all sides. Drain on paper towels.

The Williamson Family, Lafayette

Pan-Fried Pecan Cayenne Catfish

1 pound catfish filets
1 cup milk
⅓ cup chopped pecans
½ cup cornmeal
¼ cup flour
2 tablespoons cayenne pepper
1 teaspoon garlic powder
1 teaspoon onion powder
1 teaspoon salt
1 teaspoon pepper
1 stick butter
¼ cup olive oil

In a bowl, soak catfish filets in milk for 15 minutes. In a shallow dish, combine remaining ingredients except butter and oil. Dredge fish evenly in dry ingredients Heat butter and olive oil in a hot skillet. Sauté fish approximately 8 minutes per side. Sprinkle remaining dry mixture over fish as it cooks.

Shark Tidbits

1 can flat beer
1 pound Louisiana shark filets
2 cups self-rising flour
¼ teaspoon basil
1 cup cornmeal
1 teaspoon salt
1 teaspoon black pepper
1½ cups milk
2 tablespoons prepared mustard
Vegetable oil

Pour beer over shark filets. Marinate 1 hour in refrigerator. In separate bowl, thoroughly mix flour, basil, cornmeal, salt and pepper. In another bowl, combine milk and prepared mustard. Blend into dry ingredients to form a smooth batter. Preheat frying pan with enough vegetable oil to cover fish at least 1 inch. Drain flat beer from shark. Coat fish with batter, letting excess batter drop back into bowl. Place fish in oil over medium heat. When fish is done, it will float and turn a light golden brown color. Serve with tartar sauce or Thousand Island dressing.

Seafood Promotion and Marketing Board

Bobbi Lynne's Fresh Catch Creole Fish & Vegetable Mélange

1 tablespoon liquid crab boil
6 cloves garlic, whole
4 new potatoes, quartered
6 baby carrots, quartered
1 rib celery, 1 inch pieces
½ mirliton (or chayote), cubed
6 mushrooms, quartered
½ cup fresh corn kernels
1 lemon
4 fresh fish filets (catfish, drum, redfish, flounder, or bass is recommended)

Cajun seasoning, to taste (Fontenot & a Half, 225.749.4049 www.fontenotandahalf.com)
White wine (for deglazing pan)
1 tablespoon garlic infused olive oil
1 cup low-sodium chicken broth
4 tablespoons Creole mustard
¼ teaspoon thyme
½ teaspoon minced dried onion
2 teaspoons red wine vinegar
1 teaspoon flour

Fill a medium saucepan halfway with water, and a medium pasta pot ¾ full of water; set both to boil. When saucepan water reaches a boil, add crab boil. Stir and remove from heat; allow to cool. When pasta pot comes to boil, add garlic and potatoes; cook about 15 minutes (or until potatoes are tender). Take half of the crab boil water and add to a bowl of ice to create an ice bath for the veggies. Remove potatoes from water, shock in the ice bath, then move to a colander to drain. Add carrots, celery, mirliton, mushrooms, corn and ½ lemon to the boiling water; cook until tender but firm (about 15 to 20 minutes). While that batch of veggies is cooking, season the fish filets liberally with the Cajun seasoning. Heat olive oil in a large sauté pan over medium heat. Add fish filets, and cook 2 to 3 minutes on each side. If fish begins to stick to pan, sprinkle a few teaspoons of white wine into the pan to loosen. Once fish is cooked, set aside on a plate and cover with aluminum foil to rest. Add chicken broth, mustard, thyme, onion, juice from the other half of the lemon, and vinegar to the sauté pan; stir well. Sprinkle in flour and whisk until thickened (about 2 minutes). While sauce is cooking, reheat the saucepan of crab boil water over medium-low heat. When veggies are done, shock in the ice bath, drain, then add all veggies back into the remaining crab boil water to reheat (about 1 minute). Drain well, season with Cajun seasoning to taste. Arrange vegetables on plate and drizzle mustard sauce over fish. Serve with a fresh warm roll.

Bobbi Lynne Shackelford, Lafayette

Cajun Shrimp Boil

½ small bottle hot sauce
½ small bottle Worcestershire sauce
1 carrot, chopped
2 onions, chopped
2 tablespoons minced garlic
2 tablespoons liquid crab boil
1 tablespoon black pepper
4 lemons, halved
4 tablespoons Cajun seasoning
2 jalapeño peppers, seeded and minced
2 bay leaves
10 small red potatoes, whole
2 pounds smoked sausage, sliced
6 ears corn, halved
5 pounds shrimp

Combine everything, except corn and shrimp, in a large pot; add water to more than cover. Bring to a boil and cook, covered, until potatoes are beginning to tender. Add in corn. Cook until potatoes are done then add shrimp. Cook until shrimp is done. Carefully drain off water, dump the finished, drained boil onto a table covered with newspaper.

Spiced-Up Tuna Casserole

1 box macaroni and cheese dinner,
    plus ingredients to prepare per directions on package
1 can cream of celery soup
1 cup frozen peas
1 can Rotel
2 cans tuna, well drained and flaked
½ cup milk
2 teaspoons chopped onion
1 can chopped green chiles
1 tablespoon hot sauce
2 teaspoons garlic powder
Salt and pepper to taste
2 cups breadcrumbs
¼ cup (½ stick) butter or margarine, melted

Prepare dinner as directed on package. Add soup, peas, Rotel, tuna, milk, onion, green chiles, hot sauce, garlic powder, salt and pepper. Mix evenly then spoon into a casserole dish. Toss crumbs and butter; sprinkle over casserole. Bake at 350° for 30 to 35 minutes or until thoroughly heated.

Danny Franklin

Cajun Hot Tuna Steaks

6 (6-ounce) tuna steaks
1 tablespoon olive oil plus more
1¼ cups white wine
1 cup cilantro leaves
1 cup unsalted butter
¼ cup minced shallots
2 tablespoons white wine vinegar
1 tablespoon horseradish
½ tablespoon hot sauce
1 tablespoon soy sauce
Salt and pepper to taste

Brush each side of each steak with olive oil and set aside. In a bowl, combine 1 tablespoon olive oil and remaining ingredients. Marinate tuna steaks, covered and chilled, about 30 minutes. Cover bottom of skillet with oil and heat. Cook steaks evenly on both sides over high heat. Cooking time will depend on thickness of cuts. Serve hot.

Grilled Tuna with Cucumber Yogurt Sauce

2 cups plain yogurt
1 tablespoon lemon juice
2 garlic cloves, minced
1 tablespoon chopped dill
Dash hot sauce
½ cucumber, peeled and diced
1 teaspoon relish
Salt and pepper
6 (8-ounce) tuna steaks
Olive oil

Combine yogurt with lemon juice, garlic, dill, hot sauce, cucumber, relish and salt and pepper to taste. Cover and chill. Brush tuna steaks with olive oil and sprinkle with salt and pepper to taste. Grill over medium-high heat or broil in the oven 15 to 20 minutes, or until fish flakes easily; turn only once. Serve hot with Cucumber Yogurt Sauce on the side.

Wayne Shackleford, Austin

QUE'IN ON THE RED

March • Alexandria

This annual barbecue competition has good food, great music, family fan, friendly competition, great prizes and much more. We offer traditional festival food as well as a taste of good southern barbecue. A children's area is filled with rides and games for a fun and exciting family event. Our People's Choice tent is always popular with the opportunity to taste and judge your favorite team entry. Join us... it's tradition.

318.449.5056 • www.queinonthered.com

Shrimp Etouffée

½ cup butter or margarine
2 medium onions, chopped
1 cup chopped celery
1 cup chopped green onions
2 cloves garlic, minced
½ cup flour
4 cups water
2 cans tomatoes, drained
2 tablespoons lemon juice
1 teaspoon salt
2 bay leaves
¼ teaspoon dried thyme leaves
2 pounds shrimp, peeled and deveined
½ teaspoon hot sauce
Hot cooked rice

Melt butter in a large saucepan; add onions, celery, green onions and garlic. Cook 5 minutes or until golden. Add flour; stir until well blended and mixed. Stir in water, tomatoes, lemon juice, salt, bay leaves and thyme. Bring to a boil, reduce heat and cover. Simmer 30 minutes, stirring occasionally. Add shrimp and hot sauce. Simmer 5 minutes longer or until shrimp turn pink. Remove bay leaves before serving. Serve hot over cooked rice.

LOUISIANA SHRIMP AND PETROLEUM FESTIVAL

Labor Day Weekend • Morgan City

This award-winning festival has been celebrated more than 70 years and is the state's oldest-chartered harvest festival. It is one in a dying breed of quality events offering family entertainment at no cost to the visitor (no gate fees are charged). The festival is also unique because nearly 40 non-profit organizations utilize it as their sole or primary source of funding. With attendance each year averaging 100,000 to 150,000 visitors, monies earned by these organizations are quite substantial and are funded back into the community in the form of scholarships and programs sponsored by schools, churches and other non-profit endeavors.

985.385.0703 • www.shrimp-petrofest.org

Shrimp in White Remoulade

1 pound large (40 count) headless shrimp,
   boiled and peeled
¾ cup mayonnaise
1½ cups Zatarain's Creole Mustard
1½ ounces capers, minced with juice
1 small onion, minced fine
¼ cup Worcestershire sauce
1 tablespoon Tabasco
Cherry tomatoes, black olives, lemon wedges for garnish

Mix all ingredients, except shrimp, blending well. Carefully fold in shrimp mixing well to coat all pieces. Let marinate in refrigerator at least 24 hours. Serve chilled on platter lined with fancy lettuce and toothpicks on the side. Garnish with cherry tomatoes, black olives and lemon wedges.

Jill Carney, Baton Rouge

Daddy's Hot Shrimp

1 egg, separated
2 tablespoons dry white wine
1 teaspoon cornstarch
¼ teaspoon salt
2 pounds medium shrimp, peeled and deveined
Vegetable oil
⅓ cup chopped green onions, divided
½ tablespoon ginger
½ cup chicken broth
2 tablespoons ketchup
¾ teaspoon hot sauce
½ teaspoon salt
½ teaspoon sugar

Dad would use shrimp, scallops, or crawfish for this dish. It came out perfect every time.

In a medium bowl, combine egg white, wine, cornstarch and salt; mix well. Add shrimp and toss to coat evenly. Cover; refrigerate 1 hour. Remove shrimp; reserve egg mixture. Heat oil over medium-high heat. Fry shrimp, a few at a time about 1 minute. Drain on paper towels. In a skillet with a few tablespoons of the heated oil or butter, add ½ of the chopped green onions and ginger to pan; stir-fry 1 minute. Stir in broth, ketchup, hot sauce, salt and sugar. Cook for a few minutes while stirring. Next, stir in reserved egg white mixture the pre-cooked shrimp and remaining ½ cup chopped green onions. Cook an additional 5 minutes. Serve hot.

The Williamson Family, Lafayette

Pan Seared Garlic Shrimp

⅓ cup butter
1½ to 2 pounds large shrimp, peeled and deveined
4 to 6 medium cloves garlic, crushed and minced
⅓ cup chopped fresh parsley
2 to 3 tablespoons lemon juice
Salt to taste

In a large skillet, heat butter over medium heat until melted. Add shrimp and garlic; sauté over medium heat turning frequently until shrimp turn pink, about 4 to 5 minutes. Edges should have just a hint of brown color. Do not over-cook or shrimp will be tough. Add parsley, lemon juice, and salt; stir well. Serve hot with seasoned rice.

Shrimp Scalloped Potatoes

4 strips bacon
⅓ cup chopped scallions
2 tablespoons butter
4 to 6 potatoes, peeled and chopped
1 can cream of mushroom
½ cup whole milk
1 teaspoon black pepper
1 teaspoon garlic powder
1 cup small shrimp, shelled and cooked
Paprika

In a large heavy skillet, cook bacon until crisp; drain and set aside. In the same skillet, cook scallions in butter until tender. Stir in potatoes, soup, milk, pepper and garlic powder. Bring to a boil, reduce heat and cover. Cook until potatoes are soft. Stir in shrimp and cook an additional 5 minutes. Crumble reserved bacon over top and sprinkle with paprika before serving.

Angie Conner & Family, Lake Charles

Baked Bayou Cheesy Spaghetti

1 pound ground beef or sausage
1 pound frozen medium shrimp,
　　peeled and deveined
1 chopped onion
1 chopped green bell pepper
1 tablespoon butter
1 can diced tomatoes w/liquid
2 (small) cans mushroom stems and pieces,
　　drained
1 (2¼-ounce) can sliced ripe olives, drained
2 teaspoons oregano
12 ounces spaghetti, cooked and drained
2 cups shredded Cheddar cheese
1 can cream of mushroom soup
¼ cup cold water
½ cup grated Parmesan cheese

This dish was my staple for church dinners. It is very hearty and filling. Hope you enjoy.

Brown and drain ground beef. Stir in frozen shrimp and set aside. In a large skillet, sauté onion and bell pepper in butter until tender. Add tomatoes, mushrooms, olives and oregano. Simmer uncovered for 10 minutes. Place half of the spaghetti in a greased 9x13-inch baking dish. Top with half of the meat mixture, then vegetable mixture. Sprinkle with 1 cup Cheddar cheese. Mix soup and water until smooth; pour over casserole. Sprinkle with Parmesan cheese. Bake uncovered at 350° for 30 to 35 minutes or until heated through.

Carol Jenkins, Louisiana native

Creole Seafood Linguine Casserole

¾ pound medium shrimp, peeled
¾ pound scallops
3 tablespoons olive oil
1 large onion, finely chopped
2 cloves garlic, minced
1 tablespoon Italian seasoning
½ cup dry white wine
2 cups canned spaghetti sauce
2 tablespoons chopped parsley
1 bay leaf, crumbled
2 teaspoons dried basil leaves
¾ teaspoon hot sauce
Salt and pepper
12 ounces linguine, cooked and drained
Creole seasoning

Clean, devein and rinse shrimp; set aside. Rinse scallops and set aside. Add oil to a large, heavy saucepan over medium-high heat; cook onion and garlic 5 minutes or until golden. Add Italian seasoning and wine; simmer until reduced by half. Stir in sauce, parsley, bay leaf, basil, hot sauce and salt and pepper to taste. Cook linguine as directed on box. Place linguine in a casserole dish coated with non-stick cooking spray. Sprinkle noodles with Creole seasoning. Spoon shrimp and scallops over top of noodles and again sprinkle with Creole seasoning. Top with sauce. Cover and bake at 350° about 20 minutes.

Shrimp and Grits

Shrimp:

2 bacon slices
1 pound medium-sized raw shrimp, peeled
    and deveined
⅛ teaspoon salt
¼ teaspoon pepper
¼ cup all-purpose flour
2 teaspoons canola oil

1 cup sliced fresh mushrooms
½ cup chopped green onions
2 garlic cloves, minced
1 cup low-sodium fat-free chicken broth
2 tablespoons fresh lemon juice
¼ teaspoon hot sauce

Cook bacon in a large nonstick skillet over medium heat until crispy. Remove bacon to drain on paper towel, reserving 1 teaspoon drippings in skillet. Sprinkle shrimp with salt and pepper; dredge in flour. Add oil to drippings in skillet. Sauté mushrooms 5 minutes or until tender. Add green onions, and sauté 2 minutes. Add shrimp and garlic; sauté 2 minutes or until shrimp are lightly browned. Stir in chicken broth, lemon juice, and hot sauce. Cook 2 more minutes, stirring to loosen particles from bottom of skillet. Spoon shrimp mixture over hot cheese grits, sprinkle with crumbled bacon.

Grits:

1 (14-ounce) can low-sodium fat-free chicken broth
1 cup fat free milk
1⅓ cups water
½ teaspoon salt
1 cup uncooked quick-cooking grits
¾ cup (3 ounces) shredded 2% reduced-fat sharp Cheddar cheese
1 cup grated Parmesan cheese
½ teaspoon hot sauce
¼ teaspoon ground white pepper

Bring broth, milk, water and salt to a boil in a medium saucepan over medium-high heat; gradually whisk in grits. Reduce heat to low and simmer, stirring occasionally, 10 minutes, or until thickened. Stir in remaining ingredients.

L. D., Morgan City

Bacon Shrimp Casserole

3 cups cooked and peeled shrimp
12 tortillas, cut in pieces
1 envelope dry onion soup mix
½ cup water
1 (10- to 12-ounce) jar salsa
1 can cream of chicken soup
1 can chopped mild green chilies
1 small onion, chopped
1 small can sliced ripe olives
½ cup sliced green olives
½ cup chopped pecans
½ cup cooked and crumbled bacon
2 cups grated Cheddar cheese

Line a 8x14-inch casserole dish with ½ of the tortillas. In a saucepan, combine soup mix, water, salsa, soup and green chilies. Heat thoroughly over medium heat. Pour half over tortilla pieces, arrange half of the shrimp over sauce. Combine onions, both kinds of olives, pecans and bacon; sprinkle over shrimp. Top with 1 cup grated cheese. Repeat layers, beginning with tortillas, then sauce, shrimp, onion mixture, and finish with cheese. Bake 30 minutes at 350°.

Shrimp, Onion & Almond Casserole

½ pound salad shrimp
1 pound pearl onions
1¼ cup butter or margarine
4 celery stalks, chopped
5 green onions, chopped
5 tablespoons flour
1 teaspoon salt
1 teaspoon hot sauce
½ teaspoon freshly ground pepper
2 cups half & half
⅔ cup sliced almonds
½ cup grated Parmesan cheese
Almonds for topping

Rinse shrimp and drain. Remove root end from each pearl onion. In a large saucepan with boiling water parboil onions for 2 minutes then rinse in cold water and remove skins. In a large skillet over medium heat, melt butter. Add celery, pearl onions and green onions; cook 5 minutes. Combine all ingredients, except almonds, in a baking dish and bake at 375° for 35 minutes or until bubbly and lightly browned. Top with almonds about 5 minutes before removing from oven. Allow to rest 5 minutes before serving. Serve hot.

Shrimp Onion Tot Casserole

½ cup butter or margarine, divided
1½ pounds small whole white onions, peeled
1½ cups sliced celery
1 small bag tater tots
2 tablespoons flour
1¾ cups milk
2 teaspoons hot sauce
¼ teaspoon salt
½ cup grated Parmesan cheese
1 (1-pound) bag shrimp, deveined
Cajun Seasoning
Paprika

Melt ¼ cup butter in a large skillet; add onions and celery. Cook 5 minutes. Add to casserole dish with onions, celery, tater tots, flour, milk, hot sauce, salt and Parmesan cheese. Bake at 350° for 30 to 40 minutes, or until onions are tender. In a small skillet, sauté shrimp in ¼ cup butter until done. Sprinkle with Cajun seasoning to taste as you cook. Serve casserole topped with shrimp. Sprinkle with paprika before serving.

BUCKTOWN SEAFOOD FESTIVAL

Last Weekend in October • Metairie

We have games, inflatables, prizes, the best food around and we crown a new king and queen of Bucktown each year. Local bands perform all weekend; no entry fee.

504.833.8224

Jill's Authentic White Beans and Shrimp with Bacon

Step One:

1 pound white northern beans
1 tablespoon granulated garlic
1 tablespoon granulated onion
1 tablespoon thyme
1 tablespoon Creole dry seasoning
1 teaspoon black pepper
1 teaspoon dry Italian seasoning

This recipe is worth the effort. It may not be what you would call easy, but the finished product is great.

Place beans in ½ gallon container. Add 4 cups water and remaining Step One ingredients. Stir well and refrigerate overnight.

Step Two:

2 (14-ounce) cans chicken stock
1 pound bacon
1 (1-pound) container Creole pre-chopped seasoning (onions, celery, bell pepper, parsley, garlic and green onions)
½ stick unsalted butter
¼ cup finely chopped fresh garlic
1 pound peeled shrimp
½ pint heavy whipping cream

Place beans in 5-quart crockpot. Add chicken stock, and cook approximately 4 hours on high or until beans are soft. Cut bacon into small pieces (semi-freezing bacon makes it cut easier) discarding ends that are only fat or saving them for other use). Sauté bacon several minutes. Add chopped seasoning and sauté another several minutes. Add to beans, and cook on low about 2 hours. Skim off any oil that has surfaced to the top. Mash about 1 cup beans and stir back in. Shortly before serving, sauté chopped garlic in butter. Add shrimp and cook several minutes until shrimp turn light pink; add to beans. Stir in heavy whipping cream slowly and mix well. Salt to taste. Serve alone or over rice.

Note: Best cooked in 5-quart crockpot but can be cooked in conventional stove-top pot.

Jill Dolese, Chalmette

Beer Battered Shrimp

1 cup flour
   plus more for dredging
2 tablespoons paprika
1 teaspoon salt
1 can beer
1 teaspoon each Worcestershire and hot sauce
Vegetable oil for frying
2 pounds shrimp, peeled and deveined
Flour for dredging
Cajun seasoning

Combine 1 cup flour, paprika and salt. Whisk in beer, Worcestershire and hot sauce. Cover and set aside 30 minutes. Heat enough oil for frying. Dredge shrimp in dry flour; dip in batter. Fry a few shrimp at a time for about 3 to 5 minutes, until golden brown. As soon as you remove shrimp from oil sprinkle with Cajun seasoning. Drain on paper towels.

Josh's Shrimp or Crawfish Boil

4 quarts water
8 lemons, halved
3 onions, quartered
2 cloves garlic, chopped
3 tablespoons Worcestershire sauce
1 celery stalk, chopped
3 cups sautérne or white wine
2 tablespoon cayenne red pepper
9 tablespoons salt (for shrimp) or 11 tablespoons salt (for crawfish)
5 pounds raw shrimp or crawfish

Bring water to a boil in a pot with a lid. Add all ingredients, except shellfish. Stir, cover, and return to boil. Add shellfish, cover and cook approximately 15 to 20 minutes.

Josh and Nicole Guthrie

MUDBUG MADNESS

Memorial Day Weekend • Shreveport

What began in 1984 as a two-day street festival in downtown Shreveport is now one of Louisiana's largest and most popular Cajun festivals, featuring renown Cajun, Zydeco, Blues and Jazz artists, mouth-watering Cajun cuisine, raucous contests, and fun for all ages. Now a four-day festival, Mudbug Madness is nationally recognized as one of the Southeast Tourism Society's Top 20 Events, drawing as many as 56,000 people in one day. Mudbug Madness created renewed interest in Louisiana's rich cultural heritage and the event's original organizers are proud to have brought a little bit of south Louisiana fun north to Shreveport.

318.222.7403 • www.mudbugmadness.com

Bernice's Crockpot Jambalaya

12 breakfast sausage links
1½ cups cooked cubed chicken
1½ cups uncooked instant rice
1 can chicken broth
2 to 3 cans water
2 tablespoons flour
1 tablespoon butter
1 teaspoon chopped fresh thyme (or ½ teaspoon dried)
1 teaspoon chili powder
⅛ teaspoon ground red pepper
½ tablespoon Cajun seasoning
1 green bell pepper, chopped
1 onion, chopped (¼ cup)
1 (14½-ounce) can stewed tomatoes, undrained
1 bay leaf
1 package frozen shelled shrimp

Cut sausages diagonally into 1-inch slices. Cook as directed on package, using deep 10-inch skillet; drain. Combine all ingredients, except shrimp, in a crockpot. Cover and cook on high for 2 hours. Stir in shrimp and cook an additional 20 minutes. Remove bay leaf. You can add water if needed.

Bernice Caulter

JAMBALAYA FESTIVAL

Memorial Day Weekend • Gonzales

The Jambalaya Festival Association, chartered in 1967, invites you to bring your family to Gonzales, Louisiana, Memorial Day weekend for the annual Jambalaya Festival. The festival features World Champion Jambalaya served daily, live music and entertainment, carnival rides, cooking contests, a variety of food and so much fun it takes four days to get it all in. Your whole family will enjoy the vast variety of food, fun, music and activities. We invite each one of you to come share this great South Louisiana festival with us. It will be a weekend you will never forget.

225.622.6234 • www.jambalayafestival.org

Crawfish Jambalaya

½ cup oil
2 large onions, diced
1 cup sliced smoked sausage
1 pound crawfish or shrimp tails
2 (8-ounce) cans tomato sauce

2 cups uncooked rice
1 tablespoon chopped garlic
1 tablespoon chopped parsley
1 tablespoon chopped green onions

Heat oil in a large pot. Add onions and cook until tender. Add sausage and fry 3 minutes. Add crawfish or shrimp and fry 5 minutes. Add tomato sauce and cook 15 minutes. Add rice and cook 20 minutes. Add water to cover 1 inch above ingredients and season to taste. Bring to a boil. Stir well, reduce heat to simmer, and cover. Cook over low heat 25 to 30 minutes, stirring occasionally. After cooked, stir in garlic, parsley and green onions. Let stand 5 minutes and serve.

Kyle LaBlanc www.crawdads.net

Boiled Crawfish

4 pounds Louisiana crawfish
1 large kettle ¾ filled with water
2 cups chopped celery
2 lemons, quartered
2 tablespoons minced garlic
3 sweet onions, chopped
1 box crab boil
6 ears corn, cut in thirds
1 dozen or more small red potatoes, rinsed

Bring water to a boil. Add all ingredients and boil 15 minutes. Remove from heat and allow to rest about 5 minutes. Strain and drain, spread over a table covered with newspaper. Serve hot with French bread or hush puppies.

Original Louisiana Crawfish Pie

6 tablespoons margarine
1 medium onion, small dice
½ cup diced bell pepper
½ cup diced celery
4 cloves garlic, minced
1 cup chopped green onion tops
4 tablespoons chopped fresh parsley
½ pound fresh mushrooms, sliced (optional)
10 tablespoons flour
3 tablespoons tomato paste
⅓ cup white wine
2 teaspoons salt
½ teaspoon each black pepper, basil, thyme, oregano
2 teaspoons Worcestershire sauce
16 drops Louisiana hot sauce
1 to 1½ cups half & half
⅓ cup chicken stock
5 ounces pepper jack cheese, grated
2 pounds crawfish tails
4 pie crusts (2 for each pie)
1 egg, beaten

In heavy 4-quart saucepan, melt margarine; add onions, bell peppers and celery. Sweat vegetables over high heat until translucent, about 5 minutes. Add garlic, green onions, parsley and mushrooms; cook about 2 to 3 minutes more, stirring occasionally. Add flour, stirring in a little at a time, to form a smooth, thick paste. Stir in tomato paste. Cook, stirring, 1 to 2 minutes. Add wine, blending in to keep smooth. Add salt, pepper, basil, thyme, oregano, Worcestershire and hot sauce; mix well. Whisk in half & half, then chicken broth. Stir and blend well. Bring mixture to a boil to thicken; reduce heat. Stir in cheese until it is melted. Add crawfish tails folding into mixture carefully. Cool to almost room temperature. Fill two prepared pie shells. Cover each with 2nd pie crust. Baste with beaten egg. Bake in preheated 400° oven 40 to 45 minutes, till crust is golden. Cool 5 minutes before cutting pie.

Jill Carney, Baton Rouge

Crawfish Pie

1½ pounds crawfish
4 tablespoons butter
2 cups chopped onion
1 cup chopped scallions
½ cup chopped celery
½ cup chopped bell pepper
3 cloves garlic, minced
¼ cup sifted flour
½ teaspoon ground cayenne pepper
1 medium jalapeno pepper, chopped
½ teaspoon salt
Pinch sugar
¼ teaspoon white pepper, or to taste
1 pie crust
Canned onion flakes for topping

Boil crawfish in unseasoned water. Drain and rinse. Melt butter in a large skillet and sauté onions, scallions, celery, bell pepper and garlic. Add flour and mix well. Remove from heat and stir in crawfish. Add cayenne, jalapeno, salt, pepper and sugar. Spoon into a 9-inch pie crust and bake at 350° for 15 to 20 minutes. Top with onion flakes before removing from oven.

Easy Crawfish Etouffée

1½ cups chopped onions
1 cup chopped bell pepper
1 cup chopped celery
2 cloves garlic
1½ sticks butter
1 can cream of celery soup
1 can Rotel tomatoes (chopped tomatoes with chilies)
2 pounds crawfish tails
Salt and pepper

Sauté onion, bell pepper, celery and garlic in butter. Add soup, tomatoes and crawfish. Cover and simmer about 30 minutes. Season with salt and pepper to taste. Add water as needed if sauce is too thick. Serve over cooked rice.

Mrs. Jake Moody, Eunice

WORLD CHAMPIONSHIP CRAWFISH ETOUFFEE COOK-OFF

Last Sunday in March • Eunice

Our World Championship Crawfish Etouffée Cook-Off is free to the public and a fun activity for the entire family. Teams compete to see who can cook the best crawfish etouffée (smothered crawfish usually served with rice). Thousands of visitors come to this annual event to view three categories of cook-off participants. Teams also compete for the Best Decorated booth and this category has proven to be more creative and hotly contested than even the cooking. Throughout the day outstanding Cajun and Zydeco bands perform for the listening delight and dancing pleasure of the spectators.

877.948.8004 • www.eunice-la.com/www.cajuntravel.com

Crawfish Au Gratin

½ cup chopped green onions
3 ribs celery, chopped
½ pound butter
4 tablespoons flour
1 large can evaporated milk
2 pounds crawfish tails
2 egg yolks
2 tablespoons sherry
Salt and pepper to taste
10 ounces (2½ cups) grated Cheddar cheese
½ cup Parmesan cheese

Sauté onions and celery in butter until soft. Add flour and blend. Add milk. Remove from heat and add remaining ingredients except cheeses. Pour into casserole dish. Top with Cheddar cheese and sprinkle Parmesan cheese on top. Bake at 350° for 15 minutes.

Kyle LaBlanc www.crawdads.net

SMOKED MEAT FESTIVAL

Last Full Weekend in June • Ville Platte

The Smoked Meat Festival is hosted by our Vietnam Veterans of America Chapter #632. In 1993 began Le Festival de la Viande Boucan'ee—a festival that showcases our Cajun heritage, distinctive cuisine, toe-tapping music and the natural beauty of the region.

337.363.6700 • www.smokedmeatfestival.com

Barbecued Crawfish

2 pounds Louisiana crawfish
   tailmeat
2 sticks butter
1 bell pepper, chopped
2 onions, chopped
8 ounces sliced fresh mushrooms
8 ounces barbecue sauce
2 tablespoons Cajun or Creole seasoning
Sliced French bread

Melt butter. Add peppers and onions and sauté until tender. Add mushrooms and barbecue sauce. Cook 2 minutes. Stir in crawfish and seasoning; simmer 5 minutes. Serve in bowls over sliced French bread. Serves 6.

Kyle LaBlanc www.crawdads.net

Craw Daddy Casserole

6 slices whole wheat bread
1 pound craw daddy (crawfish) meat, minced
1 medium onion, chopped
1 cup mayonnaise
2 tablespoons mustard
1 (5-ounce) can evaporated milk
Salt and pepper to taste
⅓ stick margarine

Break wheat bread into small pieces. Combine with meat, onions, mayonnaise, mustard and milk; stir until well blended. Refrigerate 2 hours before cooking to enhance flavor. Melt margarine in a 12x8-inch casserole dish. Add crawfish mixture. Bake at 350° for 45 minutes.

Grandmother's Crawfish Casserole

1 bell pepper, chopped
1 onion, chopped
4 cloves garlic, chopped
1 stick butter or margarine
2 pounds crawfish
2 cans cream of mushroom soup
4 cups cooked rice
2 jars jalapeno Cheez Whiz
Salt to taste

Sauté bell pepper, onion and garlic in butter until vegetables are soft but not brown. Add crawfish and cook a few minutes longer. Add soup, rice, cheese and salt to taste. Put in a buttered (or treated with nonstick spray) casserole dish (1 large or 2 medium-sized). Bake at 350° for 30 to 45 minutes, uncovered.

Kathleen Robinson, from the "Robinson & Stirling Family Recipe Collection"

LACOMBE CRAB FEST

Last Weekend in June • Lacombe

The largest crab-themed festival in the south, the Lacombe Crab Fest features nonstop live entertainment, a gumbo competition, an interactive cultural village with demonstrating artists, and games and carnival rides for the kids. Local restaurateurs team up with local nonprofit organizations to prepare and offer a variety of seafood and crab dishes and all sorts of beverages. Bring the whole family and join us for a weekend of fun and pure pleasure under the majestic live oaks of John Davis Park.

985.867.9490 • www.lacombecrabfest.com

Crawfish Cakes

1 pound minced crawfish
1 small onion, chopped
4 scallions, thinly sliced
1 cup breadcrumbs
¾ teaspoon salt
½ teaspoon black pepper
¼ teaspoon cayenne pepper
2 teaspoons lemon juice
2 eggs, lightly beaten
½ stick butter, melted
Flour
8 tablespoons butter

Combine crawfish meat in a mixing bowl with onion, scallions, breadcrumbs, spices and lemon juice. Blend while adding eggs and melted butter. Divide into ten portions and shape into small cakes. Dredge each cake lightly in the flour, and pat lightly on each side to remove all excess flour. Cook in hot butter until golden. Drain and serve.

Kettle Boiled Crabs

1 large kettle
Water (to fill kettle ¾ full)
4 tablespoons liquid crab boil
¼ cup salt
¼ cup vinegar
1 lemon sliced and squeezed into water
4 dozen live Louisiana blue crabs

Bring water, crab boil, salt, vinegar and lemon to a rolling boil. Add live crabs. Return to a rolling boil and boil 15 minutes. Remove from heat (or turn off heat source). Allow to rest about 5 to 10 minutes. Remove crabs and drain. Serve hot over a table covered in newspaper.

New Orleans Eggplant Crabcakes

2 whole eggplant
1 white onion, chopped
2 ounces chopped garlic
6 celery sticks
1 medium-sized leek, chopped
1 tablespoon thyme
1 tablespoon marjoram
3½ ounces white wine, divided
1 tablespoon olive oil plus more for cooking
2 pounds Louisiana crabmeat
1 teaspoon crushed pepperoncino (red pepper flakes)
1 cup breadcrumbs plus more for coating
½ cup Parmesan cheese

Preheat oven to 400°. Cut eggplant in half, lengthwise. Salt eggplant and layer in a baking pan. Add 1 cup water and bake 30 minutes. Remove eggplant as it becomes tender. Heat a skillet on top of the stove and add onion and garlic. Sauté until golden brown in color. Add celery, leeks, herbs, and 3 ounces (6 tablespoons) white wine; mix well. With a spoon, remove meat from eggplant. Process eggplant meat in a food processor with ingredients from skillet until mixed well. In another skillet, add olive oil, crabmeat, ½ ounce (1 tablespoon) white wine and bring to a boil. Add eggplant mixture, salt and pepper to taste and pepperoncino (red pepper flakes). Mix well; cool. Add breadcrumbs and Parmesan cheese. Roll like a patty (about 4 ounces each). Add a touch of breadcrumbs to both sides. Heat 1 ounce olive oil in a skillet and sauté patties on both sides until golden brown.

Chef Andrea Apuzzo and Seafood Promotion and Marketing Board, New Orleans

Oyster Fritters

12 oysters, shucked
Oil for frying
2 tablespoons hot sauce
2 eggs, beaten
1 can green chilies
½ cup minced onion
1 clove garlic, minced
2 cup self-rising flour
1 cup milk
½ teaspoon oregano
Sat and pepper
½ stick butter, melted

Chop oysters raw or fry them oil and then chop them. Combine with remaining ingredients and mix to a thick batter. Drop by spoonful into hot oil. Fry until golden.

Fried Oysters

12 oysters, shucked
½ cup milk
⅔ cup all-purpose flour
½ teaspoon salt
¼ teaspoon pepper
Garlic powder
Dash hot sauce
Oil for frying

Drain liquid from oysters and clean them. Place oysters in a bowl, add milk covering completely. In a separate bowl, combine flour, salt, pepper and garlic powder to taste. Drizzle each oyster with hot sauce and roll individually in flour mixture. Heat oil and fry oysters 2 to 3 minutes on each side or until browned. Serve hot.

Ben's Oysters Rockefeller

36 oysters, in shells
1 bunch spinach, washed
1 bunch green onions, tops
1 bunch parsley, stems removed
1 stalk celery, minced
½ cup butter or margarine, melted
Juice of 1 lemon
Rock Salt

Using food processor, process spinach, onion tops and parsley until fine. Mix with celery, melted butter and lemon juice. Fill 6 pie plates or tins half-full with rock salt. Place 6 oysters on half shell in each plate. Cover each oyster with 1 teaspoon vegetable mixture. Place plates under broiler; cook until edges of oysters curl, then serve immediately.

Ben and Linda Campbell, LSU football fans

LOUISIANA OYSTER JUBILEE

April • New Orleans

Started April 2006, in an effort to support Louisiana fishermen and bring tourists back to the French quarter following Hurricane Katrina, Oyster's Jubilee is truly a jubilee of oysters. Acme Oyster House fries 5,200 Louisiana oysters, and 340 feet of famous Leidenheimer French Bread is placed on tables that line an entire French Quarter block on Royal Street. More than 15 restaurants "dress" a section of the po'boy as they please. From bacon to soy sauce, no section is dressed the same. Once complete the po'boy is free for the taking, but trust me, it doesn't last long!

504.293.2647 • www.oysterjubilee.com

Cakes, Cookies & Candies

Cajun Brad Pitt Cake

1 Devils Food Cake mix
   plus ingredients to prepare per directions
1 jar caramel ice cream topping
1 (16-ounce) carton Cool Whip
2 Butterfinger candy bars, crushed

Bake cake in a 9x13-inch baking dish according to directions on box. While still warm, poke holes in cake with large fork; fill holes with caramel. Cool in refrigerator about 30 minutes. Cover with Cool Whip then sprinkle with candy. Rich and good. Enjoy.

Miss Lizzies Shop, Homer

Nicole's King Cake

Cake:

¼ cup butter or margarine
1 (16-ounce) container sour cream
⅓ cup plus 1 tablespoon sugar, divided
1 teaspoon salt

Filling:

⅓ cup butter or margarine, softened
1½ teaspoons ground cinnamon
½ cup sugar

2 (¼-ounce) pouches/envelopes
   active dry yeast
½ cup warm water
2 eggs
5½ cups flour, divided

Frosting:

3 cups powdered sugar
¼ cup lemon juice
3 to 6 tablespoons water

Cook butter, sour cream, sugar and salt in a saucepan over low heat, stirring often, until butter melts. Remove from heat to cool. In the meantime, dissolve yeast and 1 tablespoon sugar in ½ cup warm water in a large bowl; let stand 5 minutes. As the butter mixture cools, add to yeast mixture along with eggs and 2 cups flour. Beat at medium speed with electric mixer until smooth. Gradually add the rest of the flour, switching from mixer to spatula/spoon and hands as soft dough forms. Turn dough out onto a lightly-floured surface and knead until smooth and elastic. Use oil to lightly grease a bowl. Place dough in the bowl, turning once to coat all sides. Cover with a towel and place in a warm place at least 1 hour, or until it doubles in size. Punch dough down and divide it in half. Place one portion aside. Roll other half out on a lightly floured surface. You want to end with a rectangle, which is difficult if you don't begin to roll the dough that way from the beginning. Once you have the rectangle, cover the entire surface with a light cover of butter. Combine cinnamon and sugar. Sprinkle half over the entire surface. Roll entire rectangle lengthwise, jelly-roll style. Once you have a roll, bring the two sides together to form an oval. Place seam side down on a lightly greased cookie sheet. Use a little water to pinch the ends together. Repeat second half of the dough using the remaining butter and remaining cinnamon sugar. Cover ovals with a towel and let rise in a warm place for 20 minutes or until doubled in size. Bake at 375° degrees for 13 minutes or until golden brown; cool. Combine Frosting ingredients and pour over top. Use food coloring to create purple, green and yellow sugars. Before frosting dries, sprinkle colored sugar in bands around the oval.

Nicole Haase, New Orleans

Patient Coconut Cake

1 package butter cake mix
   plus ingredients to prepare per directions
2 cups sugar
1 (16-ounce) carton sour cream
1 (12-ounce) package frozen coconut, thawed
1½ cups whipped topping

This is called Patient Coconut Cake because it takes patience, but it's well worth the wait. After it's baked, seal it in an airtight container and refrigerate it 3 days before serving.

Prepare cake mix according to package directions making 2 (8-inch) layers; cool. While cake is cooking, combine sugar, sour cream and coconut blending well; chill. When cake is cooked, split each layer in half lengthwise to make 4 thin layers. Remove coconut mixture from refrigerator and reserve 1 cup for frosting. Spread remainder between cake layers. Combine reserved coconut mixture with whipped topping; mix well. Spread on top and sides of cake. Seal cake in an airtight container and refrigerate 3 days before serving.

7-Up Pound Cake

3 cups sugar
2 sticks margarine, softened
½ cup Crisco oil
5 eggs
3 cups plain flour
1 cup 7-Up (or Sprite)
2 teaspoons vanilla extract
1 teaspoon lemon extract

Cream sugar and margarine; mix in oil. Add eggs one at a time; mixing well between each. Add flour and 7-Up alternately mixing well. Add vanilla and lemon extract; beat on medium speed for 2 minutes. Pour into a greased Bundt pan. Bake at 325° for 65 to 70 minutes.

Anita Bostain, Zwolle

Party Pecan Rum Cake

Cake:

½ cup finely chopped pecans
1 box yellow cake mix
1 package vanilla instant pudding
½ cup light rum
½ cup water
½ cup vegetable oil
3 eggs, beaten
⅓ cup crushed pecans

Glaze:

¼ cup light rum
¼ cup water
1 cup sugar
½ cup (1 stick) butter

Combine cake ingredients in a bowl and mix well. Spray a bundt pan with nonstick cooking spray. Pour cake batter into prepared pan. Bake at 325° for 50 minutes. While cake is baking, make a glaze by combining rum, water, sugar and butter in a saucepan. Bring to a boil; boil 2 minutes. Cool slightly then pour over cake. Garnish with more pecans, as desired.

Angie Pentier

Special Chocolate Cake

2 cups all-purpose flour
2 cups sugar
1 teaspoon baking soda
1 teaspoon cinnamon
1 stick butter
½ cup shortening
4 tablespoons cocoa
1 cup water
½ cup buttermilk
2 eggs
1 tablespoon vanilla

Sift flour, sugar, baking soda and cinnamon together. In saucepan, bring to boil butter, shortening, cocoa and water stirring constantly. Pour over dry ingredients; beat well. Add buttermilk, eggs and vanilla while beating. Beat well and pour into a buttered 9x13-inch pan or Bundt pan. Bake at 400° for 25 to 30 minutes. Use desired icing on cooled cake.

Blanche England, Blanchard
"Something New in 92"
Poke Salad Festival Official Cookbook

Spice Cake a la Louisian

½ cup shortening
½ cup sugar
2 eggs, beaten
2½ cups all-purpose flour
1½ teaspoons soda
½ teaspoon salt
1 teaspoon ginger
1 teaspoon cinnamon
1½ cups cane syrup
1 cup boiling water
1 cup chopped nuts, optional

Cream shortening and sugar until fluffy. Add eggs, flour, soda, salt, ginger and cinnamon alternately with syrup and water. Add chopped nuts, if desired. Beat just enough to mix thoroughly. Pour batter into a 9x13-inch pan treated with non-stick spray. Bake at 350° for 45 minutes or until a toothpick inserted in the cake comes out clean.

© Natalia Bratslavsky • bigstockphoto.com

There's always a party on Bourbon Street New Orleans

Crunchy Top Buttermilk Cake

5 eggs, separated
1 cup (2 sticks) butter
3 cups sugar
3 cups flour
1 cup buttermilk
⅓ teaspoon baking soda, dissolved in 1 teaspoon hot water

Preheat oven to 350°. Beat egg whites until stiff and peaking; set aside. In a large mixing bowl, cream butter and sugar. Add egg yolks one at a time, mixing well after each. Add flour and buttermilk, alternately continue to mix well. Dissolve baking soda in 1 teaspoon hot water; add to batter. Fold in egg whites and pour into a 9x13-inch pan treated with non-stick spray. Cool and cut in 2-inch squares,. Refrigerate left-overs.

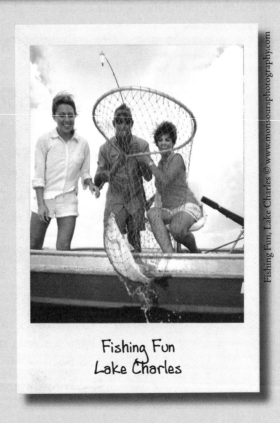

Fishing Fun, Lake Charles © www.monsourphotography.com

Fishing Fun
Lake Charles

Morganza Cake

Devils Food Cake Mix
  plus ingredients to prepare per directions

Icing:

2 cups sugar
½ cup evaporated milk
1 stick butter or margarine
1 teaspoon vanilla

Prepare cake in a 9x13-inch pan; cool. Cook first 3 icing ingredients over medium-high heat until boiling. Reduce heat but keep it at a boil; continue to boil approximately 3 minutes. Set pot in cool water and add vanilla. Beat until thick enough to spread on the cake.

Christmas Celebration & Gumbo Cookoff, Morganza

Pineapple Mardi Gras Cake

2 small cans crushed pineapple,
  drained and juice reserved
1 white cake mix plus ingredients per directions
1 can condensed milk
1 can cream of coconut
1 cup shredded coconut
1 (8-ounce) carton whipped topping

Measure juice from pineapple and add milk or water to get liquid required for on cake directions. Combine cake per directions; add pineapple. Pour into a glass baking dish. Drip different colors of food coloring over the cake batter before baking and swirl with a spoon. Bake as directed on box. Remove from oven and poke with a wooden spoon handle to make plenty of holes. Combine condensed milk and cream of coconut; pour over hot cake. Top with coconut then whipped topping. Chill before serving.

Buttercream Banana Cupcakes

1½ cups flour
1½ teaspoons baking soda
1½ teaspoons baking powder
½ teaspoon salt
1 stick butter
¾ cup packed brown sugar
1 large egg
½ cup vanilla yogurt
1 mashed banana
½ teaspoon vanilla

Frosting:

1 container buttercream frosting
1 cup powdered sugar
1 stick butter, softened
1 teaspoon vanilla extract
¼ cup milk

Preheat oven to 350°. Grease cupcake pan. Sift together first 4 ingredients, set aside. In a separate bowl, cream butter and brown sugar. Add egg. Beat in yogurt, banana and vanilla. Combine wet and dry ingredients; mix well. Pour into cupcake tin; bake 20 minutes. Cool. Combine frosting ingredients and spread over cooled cupcakes.

Lo-Fat Chocolate Éclair Cake

24 sheets graham crackers, divided
3¼ cups skim milk, divided
2 small packages fat-free vanilla instant pudding mix
1 (8-ounce) package fat-free cream cheese, softened
1 (8-ounce) carton Lite Cool Whip
2 tablespoons margarine, softened
2 tablespoons honey
2 (1-ounce) squares unsweetened baking chocolate, melted
1½ cups powdered sugar

This is a family favorite that we all have enjoyed. It's real easy.

Spray a 9x13-inch pan with nonstick spray. Place a layer graham crackers in the bottom. Combine 3 cups milk, pudding and cream cheese. Beat on low speed till thick. Fold in whipped topping. Spread half of this mixture over graham crackers. Top with another layer of graham crackers, then pudding mix, and finish with a third layer of crackers. Combine ¼ cup milk, margarine, honey and chocolate. Stir and gradually add in powdered sugar. Spread over top layer of crackers.

Amy Kirsch, Baton Rouge

Deacon Cookies

1 cup butter, softened
1 cup packed brown sugar
1 cup sugar
1 teaspoon vanilla
2 eggs
½ teaspoon baking powder
½ teaspoon salt
1 teaspoon baking soda
2 cups flour
1 cup coconut
1 cup chopped walnuts
1½ cup quick rolled oats
2 cups cornflakes
1 (12-ounce) bag butterscotch chips

My momma always called these Deacon Cookies. She made them for every church event. They were one of my favorites growing up.

Cream butter, sugars and vanilla. Add eggs, baking power, salt, soda, and flour; mix well. Stir in remaining ingredients by hand. Drop by spoonfuls on greased cookie sheet. Bake at 375° about 10 minutes. Serve fresh with cold milk.

Stephen Nash, Baton Rouge

Willie's Chocolate Chip Cookies

2¼ cups all-purpose flour
1 teaspoon baking soda
1 teaspoon salt
1 cup (2 sticks) butter, softened
¾ cup sugar
¾ cup brown sugar, packed
1 teaspoon vanilla extract
2 eggs
2 cups Nestle Tollhouse semi-sweet chocolate morsels
1 cup chopped nuts

Preheat oven to 375°. Combine flour, baking soda and salt in small bowl. In a large mixing bowl, beat butter. Add sugar, brown sugar and vanilla. Add eggs, 1 at a time, beating well after each addition. Gradually beat in flour mixture. Stir in morsels and nuts. Drop by rounded tablespoon onto ungreased baking sheets. Bake 9 to 11 minutes, or until golden brown. Cook on baking sheets 2 minutes. Remove to wire rack to cool.

Senator Willie Mount, Lake Charles

Fruit Cake Cookies

1 pound chopped dates
8 ounces candied cherries, cut into pieces
8 ounces candied pineapple, cut into pieces
1 pound pecans, chopped
1 cup butter
1½ cups sugar
2 eggs
2½ cups flour
1 teaspoon salt
1 teaspoon cinnamon

These cookies are perfect for Christmas. They look like fruit cake but have their own distinctly delicious taste.

Combine all ingredients and drop by teaspoon onto greased cookie sheet. Bake at 350° for 10 to 15 minutes. Makes 4 to 6 dozen depending on size of cookie.

Almond Macaroon Fingers

1 can almond paste
½ cup powered sugar
2 large egg whites
½ teaspoon vanilla extract
2 (1-ounce) pieces semisweet chocolate, broken into pieces

Preheat oven to 300°. Line 2 cookie sheets with parchment. Combine almond paste and sugar until mixed. Add whites and vanilla; mix well. Spoon batter into decorating bag fitted with ½-inch star tip. Squeeze batter into 3-inch-long fingers, each 1-inch apart, onto prepared cookie sheets. Bake 17 to 19 minutes or until cookies start to turn golden brown on edges. Cool on cookie sheets on wire racks. In microwave-safe bowl, heat chocolate on High 1 minute or until soft. Brush chocolate on half of each macaroon and chill 5 minutes.

Sour Cream Molasses Cookies

1 cup plus 2 tablespoons butter, softened
   (divided)
1 cup sugar
1 cup molasses
1 cup sour cream
2 teaspoons ground ginger
½ teaspoon salt
3 teaspoons baking soda
3 tablespoons white vinegar
3 eggs, beaten
4 cups sifted flour
2 cups powdered sugar, sifted
5½ tablespoons milk, warm
3 tablespoons milk, very hot
1 teaspoon lemon extract

Beat 1 cup butter and granulated sugar until light and fluffy. Stir in molasses, sour cream, ginger and salt. In a separate bowl, combine baking soda and vinegar; add to butter mixture. Beat in eggs until combined. Stir in flour. Drop by tablespoonful, 3 inches apart, onto a parchment paper-lined baking sheet. Bake at 350° until a toothpick inserted in the center comes out clean, about 15 minutes. Cool before frosting. Using a wooden spoon, beat powdered sugar, 5½ tablespoons warm milk, and remaining 2 tablespoons butter. Stir in lemon extract. Add 3 tablespoons hot milk; beat until smooth. Frost cookies, allow frosting to set before serving.

Louisiana Pecan Chocolate Cookies

2 tablespoons unsalted butter, softened
1 cup light brown sugar
1 large egg
1 teaspoon vanilla extract
¼ cup all-purpose flour
½ teaspoon baking powder
1 pinch salt
1 cup chopped pecans
8 ounces bittersweet chocolate, melted

Line baking sheets with wax paper. Using a mixer on low speed, beat butter and brown sugar until well blended. Beat in egg and vanilla. Add flour, baking powder, and salt; beat until blended. Stir in pecans. Spoon batter by teaspoonfuls onto prepared baking sheets spacing cookies about 3 inches apart. Bake 6 minutes at 350°. Cool on baking sheet 5 minutes or until firm. Dip cookies into melted chocolate or drizzle chocolate over the top. Allow chocolate to set before serving.

LOUISIANA WATERMELON FESTIVAL

Last weekend of July • Farmerville

The Louisiana Watermelon Festival offers activities from seed spitting, melon eating, the largest melon contest, melon decorating, to the melon auction. Watermelons will take over the small town of Farmerville for three fun-filled days. Thousands are expected to convene on the streets of Farmerville as the Watermelon Festival celebrates summer with great live music, classic backyard food, as well as other favorites, and a colorful mix of good time games, craft booths and activities for adults and children alike. Admission to the Festival is FREE for all.

318.368.0044 • www.lawatermelonfestival.com

Louisiana Pecan Peanut Butter Cookies

2 sticks butter, softened
1 cup packed brown sugar
1 cup plus 2 tablespoons sugar, divided
2 teaspoons vanilla extract
2 large eggs
1 (18-ounce) jar creamy peanut butter
1 cup finely chopped pecans
2 cups all-purpose flour
1 teaspoon baking powder
1 teaspoon baking soda
1 teaspoon salt

I used to pick up pecans by the bag full around my grandmother's house. I would shell them, crush them and then we would all make these great cookies.

Combine flour, baking powder, baking soda and salt. Using a mixer on medium speed, beat butter, brown sugar and 1 cup sugar until creamy, about 2 minutes. Reduce speed to low. Add vanilla. Add eggs, 1 at a time, beating well after each addition. Add peanut butter and beat on medium speed 2 minutes or until creamy. Add pecans. In a separate bowl, combine flours, baking powder, baking soda and salt. With mixer on low, beat flour mixture into peanut butter mixture just until blended. Drop dough by rounded tablespoons spaced about 2 inches apart on a large ungreased cookie sheet. Press down with a fork to make lines and sprinkle with sugar remaining 2 teaspoons sugar. Bake cookies 12 to 14 minutes at 350° or until lightly browned at edges. Cool cookies on cookie sheet 2 minutes. Transfer cookies to wire rack to cool completely.

S. Thompson, New Orleans

Chocolate Whiskey Balls

1 cup crushed vanilla wafers
¼ cup whiskey
1 cup crushed pecans
2 tablespoons white corn syrup
1 cup powdered sugar plus more for coating
1 tablespoon cocoa

Mix all ingredients well by hand. Roll into small balls, and roll in powdered sugar. Store in plastic zippered bag until serving.

Saints Butterscotch Brownies

2¼ cups all-purpose flour
1 teaspoon baking powder
¼ teaspoon salt
1 cup butter, softened
1¾ cup packed brown sugar
1 tablespoon vanilla extract
2 eggs
1 (12-ounce) package butterscotch chips, divided

This is my favorite Saints football tailgate dessert. They're Saints gold in color instead of the usual brown brownie. All my friends like them.

Preheat oven to 350º. Combine flour, baking powder, and salt in a medium bowl; set aside. In a mixing bowl, beat together butter, brown sugar, and vanilla extract until creamy. Add eggs and mix well. Gradually add flour mixture and ¾ of the butterscotch morsels. Spread into an ungreased 9x13-inch baking pan and sprinkle remaining morsels on top. Bake 30 to 40 minutes or until a toothpick or knife inserted in the center comes out clean.

Stephen Nash, Baton Rouge

Golden Cajun Brownies

1 box yellow cake mix
1 stick butter, melted
3 eggs, divided
1 (8-ounce) package cream cheese, softened
1 box powdered sugar
2 eggs, beaten until fluffy

Preheat oven to 350°. Beat 1 egg. Add cake mix and melted butter; mix well. Press into an 8x8-inch greased glass baking dish. Beat 2 remaining eggs until fluffy. Add cream cheese and sugar; mix well. Pour on top of bottom layer. Bake at 350° for 30 minutes or golden brown.

Basic Brownies

½ cup butter
2 ounces unsweetened chocolate
2 eggs
1 cup sugar
1 teaspoon vanilla
¾ cup flour
½ cup chopped nuts (optional)
½ cup chocolate chips (optional)
1 package chocolate fudge frosting

Preheat oven to 350°. Melt butter and chocolate in saucepan over low heat; remove from heat. Add sugar and vanilla and stir with a wire whisk. Add eggs and mix well. Stir in flour. Stir in chocolate chips and/or nuts if desired. Do not over mix. Spread batter evenly in a treated 8x8-inch pan, and bake 30 minutes. Do not overbake.

Dream Bars

Filling:

1 cup graham cracker crumbs
1 cup shredded coconut
1 cup chopped nuts
1 cup sugar
1 small can evaporated milk
1 egg
2 sticks butter

Crust:

1 box whole graham crackers

Frosting:

½ cup melted butter
1½ cups powdered sugar
2 teaspoons (more or less) milk

This has been a favorite for years in the Bennett family.

Combine cracker crumbs, coconut and nuts; set aside. Bring sugar, milk, egg and butter to a boil; boil until thick. Stir in nut mixture. Line bottom of cookie sheet (treated with nonstick spray) with graham crackers. Spoon filling mixture over crackers. Top with another layer of graham crackers. Combine frosting ingredients using just enough milk to reach spreading consistency. Spread over graham crackers; cool. Using lines on graham crackers, break apart.

Dale Tully, Homer

Butter Almond Toffee

1 cup chopped roasted almonds,
    divided
1 cup butter
1 cup sugar
⅓ cup brown sugar
½ teaspoon baking soda
3 ounces semi-sweet chocolate chips

Sprinkle ½ almonds on a buttered 9x13-inch pan. Melt butter in a heavy pan. Add sugars and 2 tablespoons water; mix well. Bring to a boil, stirring constantly; Cook to 300° or hard-crack stage. Remove from heat and stir in baking soda. Work FAST, before it separates. Pour over almonds in the pan. Let cool about 5 minutes. Sprinkle chocolate over toffee. Spread evenly. Cool; break into pieces. Makes about 1½ pounds.

Pecan Pralines

1½ cups sugar
¾ cup brown sugar
Pinch salt
½ cup evaporated milk
2 cup pecan pieces
1 teaspoon vanilla
½ stick butter

Combine sugars, salt and milk in a saucepan and cook over medium heat, stirring constantly, until soft ball stage (mixture should be soft and hold together when dropped in cold water). Remove from heat and add pecans, vanilla and butter. Stir well. Dish out by spoonful on wax paper.

Kyle LaBlanc www.crawdads.net

Hot Buttered Pecans

1 cup pecans
2 tablespoon unsalted butter
Hot sauce

In a skillet over moderate heat, cook pecans in butter with a few dashes of hot sauce (less or more depending on your taste). Cook 10 minutes, stirring constantly, until pecans are golden brown. Transfer to paper towel to drain.

Chocolate Covered Pecans

2 cups pecan halves
½ cup semi-sweet chocolate chips
3 tablespoon heavy cream
¼ teaspoon vanilla

Place pecans in a single layer on a microwave-safe plate. Microwave on high 1 minute, stir, and microwave another minute. Set aside. Combine chocolate chips and cream in a double boiler. Stir and cook over medium heat until melted and smooth. Add vanilla and remove from heat. Stir pecan halves into chocolate until completely coated. Remove a few pecans at a time with a slotted spoon. Separate pecan halves and place onto a waxed paper lined cookie sheet or parchment paper. Refrigerate 10 minutes to set.

Butterfinger Candy

1 large box original Wheat Thins
1 small jar crunchy peanut butter
1 package chocolate almond bark

Make sandwiches with peanut butter and wheat thins. Melt chocolate bark in microwave. Dip sandwiches in chocolate (cover completely). Lay on wax paper to cool. Taste just like Butterfinger candy. People love these.

Twyla Pugh, Homer

Chex Pecan Clusters

4 cups Rice Chex cereal
2 cups coarsely broken pretzel sticks
1 cup chopped pecans
1 (16-ounce) package vanilla-flavored candy coating
½ cup semisweet chocolate chips

Spray cookie sheet with non-stick spray or grease with shortening. In large bowl mix cereal, pretzels and pecans. In a saucepan, melt candy coating over low heat, stirring constantly. Pour over cereal mixture, stirring until coated. Spread into pan. Melt chocolate chips and drizzle over top. Cool completely before breaking into pieces to serve.

Critters Candy

1 (24-ounce) package
    white almond bark
2 small cups pretzels
2 cups nuts (pecans/walnuts)
2 cups Rice Krispies
2 cups Captain Crunch peanut butter cereal

Melt almond bark. Add pretzels, nuts, Rice Krispies and Captain Crunch. Mix well. Drop by spoonfuls on waxed paper or foil. Allow to harden before serving.

Evelyn C. White, Mayhaw Festival, Starks

Chocolate Peanut Butter Balls

1 cup creamy peanut butter
1 jar marshmallow cream
1½ cups crisp rice cereal
1 cup semisweet chocolate chips
½ cup butterscotch chips
4 teaspoons shortening
½ cup crushed peanuts

In a large bowl, combine peanut butter, marshmallow cream and cereal; mix well. Melt chocolate chips, butterscotch chips and shortening in the microwave. Add crush peanuts and stir until smooth. Roll cereal mixture into 1-inch balls. Dip in chocolate allowing excess to drip off. Place on a cookie sheet lined with waxed paper. Refrigerate until firm.

Grannies Hot Crockpot Candy

16 ounces dry roasted peanuts, unsalted
16 ounces dry roasted peanuts, salted
1 German chocolate bar
2 tablespoons red hot sauce
1 (16-ounce) bag milk chocolate chips
1½ (22- to 24-ounce) packages white almond bark

In a large crockpot, layer ingredients in order listed. Place lid on crock pot and turn temperature to low. Set timer for 2 hours. Do not peek. In 2 hours, stir to mix thoroughly. Drop by teaspoonfuls onto waxed paper. You can leave out the hot sauce if desired. It's not too hot. It's just warm and full of flavor.

Renee Hebert & Family, Lafayette

Cajun Party Nuts

1¼ cups light brown sugar
2 tablespoons light Karo syrup
2 tablespoons butter
3 teaspoons Cajun seasoning
3 cups mixed nuts

Add brown sugar, Karo, butter and Cajun seasoning to a saucepan. Cook 5 minutes over medium high heat. Remove from heat and stir in nuts; mix well. Spread evenly on wax paper. Allow to cool. Break up if stuck together and serve in a bowl.

Carnation Famous Fudge

2 tablespoons butter or margarine
⅔ cup Carnation evaporated milk
1½ cups sugar
¼ teaspoon salt
2 cups (4 ounces) miniature marshmallows
1½ cups (9 ounces) Nestle Toll House semi-sweet chocolate morsels
1 teaspoon vanilla extract
½ cup chopped pecans or walnuts

Treat an 8-inch square pan with nonstick spray or butter. In medium saucepan, combine butter, evaporated milk, sugar and salt. Bring to a boil over medium heat, stirring constantly. Boil 4 to 5 minutes, stirring constantly; remove from heat. Stir in marshmallows, morsels, vanilla and nuts. Stir vigorously 1 minute or until marshmallows melt completely. Pour into a pan. Cool. Cut into squares. Makes about 2 pounds of fudge.

Cindy D. Ezernack, Zwolle Tamale Fiesta

Louisiana Pecan Mix

5 cups cereal
   (corn or wheat chex-style cereal)
1½ cups chow mein noodles
2 cups pecans, halves or pieces
⅓ cup butter, melted
1 tablespoon parsley
1 tablespoon Cajun seasoning

Preheat oven to 325°. Combine all ingredients in a bowl. Stir until well coated. Bake 25 minutes, stirring once or twice. Cool before serving.

Pies & Other Desserts

Bananas Foster

1 cup brown sugar
¼ pound (1 stick) butter
2 bananas
½ teaspoon vanilla extract
½ teaspoon cinnamon or 1 cinnamon stick
2 ounces banana liquor
2 ounces rum, divided
Vanilla ice cream

Cook sugar and butter about 5 minutes. Add bananas; simmer another 2 minutes. Add cinnamon, vanilla flavoring, banana liquor and 1 ounce rum; simmer another 2 minutes. If flambéing, pull the sauté pan back and super heat the front edge of the pan, add another 1 ounce rum with a jigger (do not pour out of the bottle). Light with a long match or roll the flame over the edge of the pan if using gas. Jiggling the sauté pan will increase the flame. Serve immediately over vanilla ice cream.

Banana Cream Pie

2 cups cold milk
2 packages vanilla instant pudding
1 (16-ounce) carton Cool Whip, divided
1 banana, sliced
1 graham cracker pie crust

An easy version of a classic recipe.

Combine milk and putting; beat with wire whisk for 2 minutes. Stir in ½ Cool Whip. Place sliced bananas in crust. Refrigerate 4 hours. Top with remaining Cool Whip and serve.

Chris Bellas' Chocolate Chip Pie

2 eggs, slightly beaten
1 stick butter, melted
1 cup chopped pecans
1 cup semi-sweet or mild chocolate chips
1 teaspoon vanilla
¼ cup all-purpose flour
1 pie crust, lightly baked

Combine all ingredients, except pie crust, and pour into pie crust. Bake at 325° for 40 to 45 minutes.

Kathleen Robinson from the "Robinson & Stirling Family Recipe Collection"

SQUIRE CREEK LOUISIANA PEACH FESTIVAL

Fourth weekend in June • Ruston

The Squire Creek Louisiana Peach Festival is a family-oriented event held annually the fourth weekend in June in Ruston. Events include arts and crafts; food; music; parade; 5K run; cookery contest; tennis, golf, and fishing tournaments; rodeo, pet show; antique car show; kids' events; fine-arts show; and more. Some events free, others, admission applies. Oldest continuous agriculture festival in Louisiana.

318.255.2031 • www.louisianapeachfestival.org

From Mama to Me Sweet Dough Custard Pie

Dough:

6 eggs
3 cups sugar
2 tablespoons vanilla extract
1 cup warm milk
9 cups all-purpose flour, divided
6 teaspoons baking powder

This is an old recipe handed down by my Mother's Mother.

Combine dough ingredients and mix well. Divide into 8 equal portions and roll each to cover 9-inch pie. Makes 8 pie shells.

Custard Filling:

6 cups whole milk
3 cans evaporated milk
6 eggs
3 cups sugar
4 teaspoons vanilla extract
2 cups cornstarch

In thick pot, bring both milks to a full boil. Combine eggs, sugar and vanilla in a bowl; beat until mixture is smooth. Add to heated milk and stir until well dissolved. Mix cornstarch with warm water until well dissolved; add to ingredients in pot. Stir constantly until thick. Pour into pie 4 shells. Use other 4 pie shells to make strips to place over filling—3 length-wise and 2 across. (This will keep the filling from boiling over.) Cook in oven at 350° approximately 40 minutes. Cool before serving.

S/T.C. Cary, President Buggy Festival in Church Point
Church Point holds the title of "Buggy Capital" of Louisiana

Chocolate Pecan Pie

4 ounces semisweet chocolate,
　chopped
¼ stick butter
½ cup dark brown sugar
3 large eggs
¼ teaspoon salt
¾ cup light corn syrup
1½ cups pecan pieces, lightly toasted
1 frozen pie crust, thawed

Stir chocolate and butter in heavy saucepan over low heat until melted. Cool slightly. Whisk brown sugar, eggs and salt. Add corn syrup and chocolate mixture; whisk. Sprinkle pecans over unbaked crust; add filling. Bake at 350° until crust is golden and filling is puffed, about 55 minutes.

Voodoo Pecan Pie

⅓ plus ¼ cup sugar, divided
1 (8-ounce) package cream cheese, softened
4 eggs, divided
2 teaspoons vanilla extract, divided
¼ teaspoon salt
1 (9-inch) pie shell, unbaked
1⅓ cups chopped pecans
1 cup light corn syrup

Combine ⅓ cup sugar and cream cheese in a bowl. Beat at high speed with a mixer until fluffy. Add 1 egg, 1 teaspoon vanilla and ¼ teaspoon salt. Blend well. Pour into pie shell. Sprinkle pecans evenly over cream cheese mixture. In a bowl, combine corn syrup, ¼ cup sugar, 3 beaten eggs and 1 teaspoon vanilla, mixing well. Carefully pour mixture over pecan layer. Bake at 375° for 35 to 40 minutes or until set. Allow to cool completely, then refrigerate at least 2 hours before serving.

Stephen Nash, Baton Rouge

Mayhaw-Pecan Tarts

Cream Cheese Pastry:

1 (3-ounce) package cream cheese, softened
1 stick margarine, softened
1 cup flour (maybe slightly more)

Blend cream cheese and margarine; stir in flour and mix until smooth. Form into ¾-inch marble-sized balls. Press each into small muffin tins. Fill with Mayhaw-Pecan Pie Filling.

Mayhaw-Pecan Pie Filling:

½ cup sugar
1 cup mayhaw syrup (or melted jelly)
½ stick margarine
3 eggs, beaten
½ teaspoon vanilla
1 cup chopped pecans

Mix sugar, syrup and margarine; beat over low heat until sugar is dissolved. Gradually add warm mixture to beaten eggs and vanilla. Put a few chopped pecans in unbaked tart shells; pour mixture over to ⅔ full. Bake at 350° about 25 minutes. (This filling works for a pie, too. Add pecans to pastry shell and pour filling over top. Bake as usual.) Freezes well.

Mayhaw Festival, Starks

Traditional Pecan Pie

3 eggs, lightly beaten
½ cup sugar
1 tablespoon brown sugar
½ teaspoon salt
2 tablespoons butter, melted
1 teaspoon vanilla extract
¾ cup dark corn syrup
2 cups pecans
1 pie shell

Combine eggs, sugar, brown sugar, salt, butter, vanilla and corn syrup in a bowl and mix well. Stir in pecans. Pour into pie shell. Bake at 325° for 60 minutes.

STARKS MAYHAW FESTIVAL

Third Weekend in June • Starks

Mayhaw jelly, Mayhaw butter, Mayhaw berries... it must be time for the Starks Mayhaw Festival. Try your hand at jelly-making and catch a glimpse of the Mayhaw Queen and her court. This family-friendly festival has carnival rides for the kids... and live entertainment for kids at heart. You'll enjoy lots of food, craft, and game booths as well as lots of Southwest Louisiana fare. Hot biscuits and Mayhaw jelly are served Saturday morning with fresh-churned butter. A jelly making demonstration is also held. Mayhaw trees, berries juice, and jelly are available. There will be plenty to go around so join us.

337.743.6297

Miss Anne's Baked Apple Dumplings

2 large sweet apples
1½ cups sugar
2½ teaspoons cinnamon
2 sticks butter, melted
Pecans, chopped
2 cans crescent rolls
1 can lemon-lime soda

This is my aunt's recipe. Everyone called her Miss Anne and she always made this for every event. She gave me the recipe before she passed. She would be happy to know it is being shared. I hope you enjoy it.

Peel and cut each apple into 8 pieces; set aside. Combine sugar, cinnamon and melted butter; set aside. Roll one piece of apple and some chopped pecans inside each crescent roll. Pinch edges to seal and place each, evenly spaced, in a baking dish. Spoon sugar mixture over top. Very gently pour lemon-lime soda over top of sugar mixture. Top with a few chopped pecans. Bake at 350° for 35 minutes or until brown.

S. Thompson, New Orleans

Peach Cobbler

2 (29-ounce) cans sliced peaches
    (cheaper the better)
White or yellow cake mix
Cinnamon
1 stick butter

Pour peaches in Dutch Oven. Add about 2 tablespoons cake mix; stir. Sprinkle remaining cake mix over the top. Sprinkle with cinnamon to taste. Pat butter over top. Bake at 350° (5 to 6 coals on the bottom and full coals on top).

Kent Hogan, DOG (Dutch Oven Gathering 318.368.8441)
Lake Darbonne State Park, Farmerville

Mel Tillis' Mother's Blueberry Cobbler

1 stick butter
2 cups flour
2 cups milk
2 cups sugar (plus more for top, if desired)
2 cups blueberries (blackberries can be used)

Melt butter in a 9x13-inch baking pan. Combine flour, and sugar; pour over melted butter. Spread blueberries over top of batter. Bake at 425° until brown. Sprinkle sugar on top, if desired, and enjoy!

Cindy D. Ezernack
Zwolle Tamale Fiesta

RED, WHITE & BLUEBERRY FESTIVAL

July 3rd & 4th • Clinton

Make plans to celebrate Independence Day with Main Street in Clinton. You'll enjoy live music, street dancing, a patriotic program and fireworks, children's games with prizes, inflatable amusements, gospel choirs, and a blueberry cooking contest. Enjoy our community spirit and celebrate with our great businesses and over 100 food and craft vendors. Blueberries and blueberry products will be available–pies, cobblers, jellies, and more. There is fun for all ages.

225.603.9003 • www.clintonla.com

Watermelon in a Blanket

12 pre-made or purchased crepes
2 tablespoons cinnamon sugar (½ cinnamon; ½ sugar)
12 (1-inch by 8-inch) seedless watermelon "logs",
    drained to remove excess moisture
Vanilla and lemon yogurt for dipping

Sprinkle one side of each crepe with cinnamon sugar and place a watermelon log at the end of each. Roll up and serve immediately with flavored yogurts for dipping. Serves 12.

Beauregard Watermelon Festival, DeRidder

Snow Capped Mountains

12 (3- to 4-inch tall) seedless watermelon,
    cut in pyramid shapes
Sweetened whipped cream
8 to 12 ounces white chocolate, shaved
¾ cup sweetened shredded coconut

Arrange 3 pyramids on each of 4 serving plates. Top with whipped cream. Decorate with the white chocolate and shredded coconut; serve. Serves 4.

Beauregard Watermelon Festival, DeRidder

Easy Bayou Ice Cream

2-liter bottle Pop Rouge cream soda
  or Barq's root beer, other types of soda can be substituted
2 cans sweetened condensed milk

Mix and pour into ice cream freezer and freeze. The ice cream tastes like an old-fashioned ice cream float.

**Thea Lobell, Ph.D.,
Keynote Speaker, Baton Rouge**

Liz's Death by Chocolate

1 chocolate cake mix
  plus ingredients to prepare per package directions
1 cup Kahlua
4 boxes Jello chocolate mousse
  plus milk to prepare per package directions
2 (12-ounce) tubs whipped topping
6 Skor candy bars, broken into small pieces

Bake cake according to package directions for a 9x13-inch cake. While cake is still hot, prick top with fork then pour Kahlua over. Let this soak in; it can be left this way overnight. Make chocolate mousse according to package directions. Crumble ½ cake and place it on bottom of large glass bowl. Layer ½ mousse, then ½ whipped topping and ½ Skor candy bars. Repeat layers. Serves 18.

Kathleen Robinson from the "Robinson & Stirling Family Recipe Collection"

Louisiana Festivals

The following is a list of more than 250 annual festivals found throughout Louisiana. Chances are, we've neglected to include some events. If you are aware of any we missed, call us toll-free 1.888.854.5954; we'll do our best to include any missed festivals in a subsequent printing. Keep in mind that dates and venues change. Please verify all information before making plans to attend any of these events. Festivals are listed alphabetically by the city where the festival is held. Call the telephone number listed or visit the festival's website for more information.

Abbeville • Daylily Festival
May • 337.893.2491

Abbeville • LA Cattle Festival & Fair
October • 337.652.0646
louisianacattlefestival.org

Abbeville • Giant Omelette Celebration
November • giantomelette.org

Abita Springs • Louisiana Bicycle Festival
June • 985.892.2624

Albany • Hungarian Harvest Dance
October • magyars.org

Amite • Oyster Festival
March • 985.748.7156
amiteoysterfestival.org

Amite • Tangipahoa Parish Free Fair
September • 985.517.2044

Angie • Great Southern Bluegrass Event
April • 985.516.4680

Arnaudville • Etouffee Festival
April • 337.754.5912

Ashland • Spring Festival
March • 318.544.0044

Baker • Buffalo Festival
August/September • 225.778.0300
cityofbakerla.us

Basile • Louisiana Swine Festival
November • 337.432.6807
laswinefestival.com

Baton Rouge • Jewish Film Festival
January • 225.927.7904 • brjff.com

Baton Rouge • Blues Festival
April • 225.383.0968 • batonrougefestival.org

Baton Rouge • Red Stick
International Animation Festival
April • 225.389.7182 • redstickfestival.org

Baton Rouge • FestForAll
May • 800.LA.Rouge ext 502
baton-rouge.com

Baton Rouge • Pennington
Balloon Championship
August • 225.933.2027 • laballooning.com

Baton Rouge • Downtown
Festival of Lights
December • downtownbatonrouge.org

Bayou Lafourche • French Food Festival
October • 985.693.7355 • bayoucivicclub.org

Belle Chasse • Plaquemine Parish
Heritage and Seafood Festival
Memorial Day Weekend • 504.394.6328
plaqueminesparishfestival.com

Belle Chasse • The Plaquemines Parish
Fair & Orange Festival
December • 504.656.7599 • orangefestival.com

Bernice • Corney Creek Festival
April • 318.285.9071 • bernicela.org

Blanchard • Annual Poke Salad Festival
May • 318.309.2647 318.929.7574
PokeSaladFestival.com

Bogalusa • Spring Festival in the Park
April • 985.735.5731

Bourg • Grand Bois Swamp
Pop/Cajun/Zydeco Fest
October • 985.594.7410

Breaux Bridge • Crawfish Festival
May • 337.332.6655 • bbcrawfest.com

Bridge City • Gumbo Festival
October • 504.329.4279 • gumbofestival.org

Bunkie • Louisiana Corn Festival
June • 800.833.4195 • bunkie.org

Calcasieu Parish • Christmas
Lighting Festival
December • 800.456.7952
visitlakecharles.org

Chalmette • Tomato Festival
May • 504.271.2953 • olpsschool.org

Chauvin • Blessing of the Shrimp Fleet &
Family Fun Day
April • 985-475-5428

Church Point • Courir de Mardi Gras
February • churchpointmardigras.com

Church Point • Cajun Woodstock for
St. Jude's Children's Hospital
April • 337.280.8710 • cajunwoodstock.com

Church Point • Buggy Festival
June • 337.684.2739
churchpointbuggyfestival.com

Clinton • Red, White
& Blueberry Festival
July • 225.603.9003 • clintonla.com

Columbia • Riverboat Festival
May • 318.649.0726 • caldwellchamber.com

Coushatta • Red River Parish
Fair & Rodeo
September • 318.932.5105

Covington • St. Tammany Parish Fair
September • 985.892.8421
sttammanyparishfair.info

Covington • Three Rivers Art Festival
November • 985.871.4141
threeriversartfestival.com

Crowley • International Rice Festival
October • 337.783.3067 • ricefestival.com

Cut Off • Cut Off Youth Center Fair
November • 985.632.7616

Delcambre • Shrimp Festival
August • 337.685.2653 • shrimpfestival.net

DeQuincy • Louisiana Railroad Days
April • 800.456.7952 • visitlakecharles.org

DeRidder • Pine Hill Trade Days
February • 337.463.4095

DeRidder • Battle of Hickory Creek Civil
War Reenactment
February • 337-375-1870
confederateveterans.com

DeRidder • Louisiana Doll Festival
April • cityofderidder.org

DeRidder • Beauregard
Watermelon Festival
June • 800.738.5534 • beauparish.org

DeRidder • Christmas in the Park
December • 337.463.2762

Destrehan • Spring Festival
April • 985.764.9315 • destrehanplantation.org

Destrehan • Plantation Fall Festival
November • 985.764.9315
destrehanplantation.org

Donaldsonville • Sunshine Festival
October • 225.473.4814
donaldsonvillecoc.org

Erath • Old Timers Days Festival
April • 615.446.2359
louisianafairsandfestivals.com

Erath • 4th of July Celebration
July • 337.937.5393 • vermilion.org

Eunice • La Cajun
Culture and Music Club
January • 337.457.2565 • eunice-la.com

Eunice • Eunice Mardi Gras Celebration
Day before Ash Wednesday • 337.457.2565
eunice-la.com

Eunice • World Championship
Crawfish Etouffee Cook-off
March • 337.457.2565 • 877.948.8004
eunice-la.com cajuntravel.com

Evangeline • Oil & Gas Festival
September • 337.824.4995
oilandgasfestival.com

Evangeline Parish • Dewey Balfa
Cajun and Creole Heritage Week
April • lafolkroots.org

Farmerville • Louisiana
Watermelon Festival
July • 318.368.0044 • lawatermelonfestival.com

Ferriday • Delta Music Festival
April • 318-757-9999 • sos.louisiana.gov/dmm

Florien • Florien Freestate Festival
November • 800.358.7802
toledobendlakecountry.com

Forest Hill • Louisiana Nursery Festival
March • 318.748.6300
louisiananurseryfestival.com

Franklin • Bayou Teche
Bear & Birding Festival
April • 225.763.5425 • bbcc.org

French Settlement • Creole Festival
October • 225.975.0530

Galiano • Golden Meadow
Firemen's Family Fishing Rodeo
September • 985.632.3800

Garyville • Frisco Fest
March • 888.322.1756

Gheens • Gheen's Bon Mange' Festival
June • 985.532.5694

Gibsland • Jonquil Jubilee
March • 318.843.6228 • jonquiljubilee.com

Gilliam • Sunflower Trail & Festival
June • 318.296.4393

Gonzales • Jambalaya Festival
Memorial Day Weekend • 225.622.6234
jambalayafestival.org

Greenburg • St. Helena Parish Forest
Festival • September • 225.222.4632

Greenwood • Pioneer Heritage Festival
September • 318.938.6930
greenwoodlachamberofcommerce.com

Gretna • Gretna Heritage Festival
October • 504.361.7748 • gretnafest.com

Hackberry • Marshland Festival
August • 337.762.3554
marshlandfestival.com

Hammond • The Smokin'
Blues & BBQ Challenge
March • 985.419.9863
hammondbluesandbbq.com

Hammond • Hammond Fest
April • hammondchamber.org

Harahan • St. Rita Pecan Festival
November • 504.733.2915
stritaharahan.com

Homer • Claiborne Parish
Christmas Festival
November • 318.927.9009 • claiborneone.org

Houma • Downtown Family Fun Fest
November • 985.873.9622

Houma • Southdown Marketplace
November • 985.851.0154
southdownmuseum.org

Independence • Italian Festival
April • 985.878.3960 • theitalianfest.com

Iowa • Iowa Rabbit Festival
March • 337.433.8475 • iowarabbitfestival.org

Jackson • Jackson Assembly
Antiques Festival and Tour
March • 225.634.7155 • felicianatourism.org

Jackson • Highland Games of Louisiana
November • 225.927.2944
lahighlandgames.com

Jeanerette • Jeanerette Creole Festival
March • 337.276.3615

Jonesboro • Sunshine Festival
and Antique Show
April • 318.259.4249
jacksonparishchamber.org

Kaplan • Louisiana Cajun Food Fest
October • 337.643.2400 • kaplanchamber.org

Lacombe • Lacombe Crab Fest
June • 985.867.9490 • lacombecrabfest.com

Lafayette • Le Festival de
Mardi Gras a Lafayette
February • 800.346.1958 • swmardigras.com

Lafayette • Festival des Fleurs de
April • 337.482.5339 • inhc.louisiana.edu

Lafayette • Festival
International de Louisiane
April • 337.232.8086
festivalinternational.com

Lafayette • LeCajun French Music
Association Festival
August • 337.367.1526
cajunfrenchmusic.org

Lafayette • Festivals Acadiens
Bayou Food Festival
October • festivalsacadiens.com

Lafayette • Boudin Cook-Off
October • boudincookoff.com

Lake Arthur • Southwest
Louisiana Migration Sensation
April • 337.774.3453 • losbird.org

Lake Charles • Western Heritage Days
January • 800.456.7952 • visitlakecharles.org

Lake Charles • Martin Luther King, Jr.
Coalition Festival
January • 800.456.7952 • visitlakecharles.org

Lake Charles • Mardi Gras
of Southwest Louisiana
January/February • 800.456.7952
swlamardigras.com

Lake Charles • Black Heritage Festival
March • 337.488.0567 • bhflc.org

Lake Charles • Southwest Louisiana
Garden Festival
March • 800.456.7952 • gardenfest.org

Lake Charles • Celtic Nations Heritage
Festival • March • 800.456.7952
celticnationsfestival.org

Lake Charles • Contraband Days
Pirate Festival
April/May • 800.456.7952
contrabanddays.com

Lake Charles • Juneteenth
June • 800.456.7952 • visitlakecharles.org

Lake Charles • Cajun Music
and Food Festival
July • 337.562.9156 • cfmalakecharles.org

Lake Charles • La Familia Festival
September • 800.456.7952
visitlakecharles.org

Lake Charles • Arts Fest
October • 800.456.7952 • visitlakecharles.org

LaPlace • St. Joan of Arc Spring Festival
April • 985.651.8279 • sjachurch.com

LaPlace • Andouille Festival
October • 985.652.9569
andouillefestival.com

LaPlace • St. John Parish
Andouille Festival
October • sjbparish.com

Larose • Family Fun Festival
April • 985.693.7355
lafourchechamber.com bayoucivicclub.org

Larose • Cajun Heritage Festival
September • 985.537.7701

Larose • A Bayou Christmas
December • 985.693.7355 • bayoucivicclub.org

Lecompte • Lecompte Pie Festival
October • 318.776.5488
asliceoflouisiana.com

Leesville • May Fest
May • 337.238.0783
venturevernon.com

Libuse • Czech Heritage Days
March • 318.466.3196

Livingston • Livingston Parish Fair
October • 225.275.5000 ext. 6623
livingstonparish.com

Logansport • River City Festival
May • 318.645.6601

Luling • Alligator Festival
September • 985.308.0204
stcharlesrotary.com

Lutcher • Festival of the Bonfires
December • 225.869.6023
festivalofthebonfires.org

Lydia • Lydia Cajun Food Fest
September • 337.230.6730 337.519.9593

Madisonville • Acoustic String Jam
Festival • April • 985-264-9952

Mamou • Mamou Cajun Music Festival
September • 337.468.2370
mamoucajunmusicfestival.com

Mandeville • Great Louisiana BirdFest
April • 985.626.1238 • northlakenature.org

Mandeville • Seafood Festival
July • 985.624.9762 • seafoodfest.com

Mansfield • Cajun Crossroads Festival
June • 318.453.3230

Many • Sabine Fair, Festival and Rodeo
September • 318.586.7062

Marion • Sportsman's Paradise Fall
Festival • October • townofmarionla.com

Marthaville • Good Ole Days
September • 318.472.6707

Merryville • Heritage Festival
March • 337.825.8118 337.825.1045
merryville.us

Metairie • Greater New Orleans
Floral Trail • June • 504.455.7419

Metairie • Bucktown Seafood Festival
October • 504.833.8224

Minden • Spring Arts Festival
April • 318.393.5991 • artsinminden.com

Minden • Scottish Tartan Festival
April • 318.207.1161

Minden • Germantown Bluegrass
Festival • September • 318.377.6061
sabinebluegrass.com

Monroe • DeltaFest
October • 318.329.4947
discoverourtown.com

Morgan City • Louisiana
Shrimp and Petroleum Festival
Labor Day Weekend • 985.385.0703
shrimp-petrofest.org

Morganza • Christmas Parade
and Gumbo CookOff
December • 225.694.3655

Moss Bluff • Moss Bluff Harvest Festival
November • 800.456.7952
visitlakecharles.org

Natchitoches • Jazz/R&B Festival
April • 800.259.1714 • natchjazzfest.com

Natchitoches • Spring Fling
May • 318.352.8394

Natchitoches • Melrose
Arts and Crafts Festival
June • 318.352.8072
historicnatchitoches.com

Natchitoches • Natchitoches-NSU
Folk Festival
July • 318.357.4332 • nsula.edu/folklife

Natchitoches • Christmas Festival
November • 800.259.1714
christmasfestival.com

New Iberia • Cajun Hot Sauce Festival
April • 337.365.7539 • sugarena.com

New Iberia • Grillin' in the Park Southwest La. Barbeque Championship Cookoff • April • 337.367.7388

New Iberia • Acadiana AirFest
May • 888.942.3742 • AcadianaAirFest.com

New Iberia • Cajun Fun Fest
May • 888.FUN.CAJUN
cityofnewiberia.com

New Iberia • Bunk Johnson
Jazz, Arts and Heritage Festival
May • 888.942.3742 • bunkjohnson.org.

New Iberia • Festival of Riches Square
Dance Festival • August • 337.364.6284

New Iberia • Halloween Festival
October • 888.942.3742

New Iberia • World Championship
Gumbo Cookoff
October • 337.364.1836 • iberiachamber.org

New Iberia • The Great Chili Challenge
November • 337.364.2273

New Iberia • Brudley's Wild Game, Seafood & Jambalaya Cook-Off
November • 337.268.9555 x100
bgcacadiana.com

New Orleans • Mardi Gras
February • mardigrasneworleans.com

New Orleans • Zulu Lundi Gras Festival
February • 504.827.1661 • lundigrasfestival.com

New Orleans • St. Joseph's Day Parade
March • ItalianAmericanMarchingClub.org

New Orleans • New Orleans
Jazz & Heritage Festival
April • 504.410.4100 • nojazzfest.com

New Orleans • Louisiana Oyster Jubilee
April • 504.293.2647 • oysterjubilee.com

New Orleans • French Quarter Festival
April • 800.673.5725 • fqfi.org

New Orleans • Freret Street Festival
April • 504.638.2589 • freretmarket.org

New Orleans • Greek Festival
May • 504.282.0259 • greekfestnola.com

New Orleans • Shakespeare Festival
at Tulane • May • 504.865.5105
neworleansshakespeare.com

New Orleans • Wine & Food Experience
May • 504.529.9463 • nowfe.com

New Orleans • Creole Tomato Festival,
Cajun-Zydeco Festival and Louisiana
Seafood Festival • June • 504.286.8735
frenchmarket.org • louisianaseafood.com

New Orleans • Cane River
Zydeco Festival
June • 504.558.6100 • jazzandheritage.org

New Orleans • Running of the Bulls
in New Orleans
July • 504.247.3714 • nolabulls.com

New Orleans • GO 4th on the RIVER
Dueling Barges Fireworks Extravaganza
July • 985.630.4604 • Go4thOnTheRiver.com

New Orleans • Essence Fest
July • 800.488.5252 • neworleansonline.com

New Orleans • Satchmo SummerFest
August • 504.522.5730 • fqfi.org

New Orleans • Voodoo Music Festival
October • voodoomusicfest.com

New Orleans • Words & Music Festival
November • 504.586.1609
wordsandmusic.org

New Orleans • Bayou Bacchanal
November • 504.341.5939
BayouBacchanal.org

New Orleans • Louisiana Swamp Festival
November • 504.861.2537
auduboninstitute.org

New Orleans • Christmas
New Orleans Style
December • 504.522.5730 • fqfi.org

New Orleans Zoo • Soul Fest
March • 800.774.7394 • auduboninstitute.org

New Orleans Zoo • Earth Fest
March • 800.774.7394 • auduboninstitute.org

New Orleans Zoo • Mother's Day
Celebration
May • 800.774.7394 • auduboninstitute.org

New Orleans Zoo • Asian Pacific
American Society Heritage Festival
May • 800.774.7394 • auduboninstitute.org

Norco • River Parishes Fall Festival
November • sacredheartschoolnorco.org

Oil City • Christmas on Caddo
Fireworks Festival
December • 318.375.5689

Olla • Central Louisiana
BlueGrass Festival
April • 318.495.7988 • sabinebluegrass.com

Opelousas • Spice & Music Festival
June • 337.948.5227 • cityofopelousas.com

Opelousas • Creole Zydeco Festival
September • 337.394.4635 • zydeco.org

Opelousas • Yambilee
October • 337.948.8845 • yambilee.com

Palmetto • Village Collage-Palmetto
Arts Festival • April • 337.623.4426

Patterson • Cypress Sawmill Festival
April • 800.256.2931 • cypresssawmill.com

Paulina • Chanel School Spring Festival
March • 225.869.5751

Pine Prairie • Boggy Bayou Fest
April • 337.599.2031 337.599.3370

Plaisance • Southwest Louisiana
Zydeco Music Festival
September • 337.232.7672 • Zydeco.org

Plaquemine • International Acadian
Festival
October • 225.964.3609 • kc970.org

Pleasant Hill • Battle of Pleasant Hill
April • 504.452.1660 504.796.2208

Pollock • Grant Parish Dogwood Festival
April • 318.765.3796 • grantcoc.org

Ponchatoula • Strawberry Festival
April • 800.917.7045 • lastrawberryfestival.com

Ponchatoula • Strawberry
Jam'n Toast to the Arts
May • 985.974.0630 • strawberryjam.org

Port Allen • Oldies But Goodies Fest
& Smokin' Oldies BBQ Cook-Off
October • 225.344.2920 • westbatonrouge.net

Port Barre • Lions Club Cracklin Festival
November • 337.585.6673
portbarrecracklinfestival.com

Ragley • Heritage & Timber Festival
October • 800.456.7952 • visitlakecharles.org

Rayne • Frog Festival
November • 337.334.2332
raynechamber.org

Robeline • Robeline Heritage Festival
October • 318.332.4968
robelineheritage.org

Robert • Louisiana Renaissance Festival
November • 866.249.1138 • la-renfest.com

Rodessa • Boomtown Days Festival
September • 318.223.4211

Ruston • Squire Creek Louisiana Peach
Festival • June • 318.255.2031
louisianapeachfestival.org

Shreveport • African American History
Month Parade and Festival
February • 318.632.5887 318.635.2923

Shreveport • Holiday in Dixie
April • 318.865.5555 • holidayindixie.org

Shreveport • Mudbug Madness
Memorial Day Weekend • 318.222.7403
mudbugmadness.com

Shreveport • ArtBreak
May • 318.673.6500 • shrevearts.org

Shreveport • Lead Belly Blues Festival
May • 877.752.3559
leadbellybluesfestival.com

Shreveport • Cinco de Mayo Fiesta
May • 318.688.5553 • louisianalulac.org

Shreveport • Let the Good Times
Roll Festival
June • 318.470.3890 • rhoomega.com

Shreveport • James Burton International
Guitar Festival • August • 318.424.5000
jamesburtonmusic.com

Shreveport • Red River
Revel Arts Festival
October • 318.424.4000 • redriverrevel.com

Sikes • Wolf Creek Festival
September • 318.628.2392

Simmesport • Atchafalaya River Festival
April • 800.833.4195

Slidell • Slidell Heritage Festival
July • slidellheritagefest.org

Slidell • Ozone Camellia Festival
December • 985. 646.0014

Sorrento • The Deep South Crane And
Rigging Swamp Pop Music Festival
July • 877.753.9990
swamppopmusicfest.com

Springhill • Lumberjack Festival
October • 318.539.5681

St. Francisville • Audubon Pilgrimage
March • 225.635.6330
audubonpilgrimage.info

St. Francisville • Audubon
Country BirdFest
April • 800.488.6502 • audubonbirdfest.com

St. Francisville • Feliciana
Hummingbird Celebration
July • 800.488.6502 • audubonbirdfest.com

St. Francisville • Camellias
in the Country
July • 800.488.6502 • audubonbirdfest.com

St. Francisville • Christmas in the
Country • December • 225.635.6330
stfrancisvillefestivals.com

St. Martinville • La Grande
Boucherie des Cajuns
February • 888.677.7200 • descajuns.com

St. Martinville • Kiwanis
St. Martinville Pepper Festival
October • 337.394.9396 • pepperfestival.org

Starks • Starks Mayhaw Festival
June • 337.743.6297

Stonewall • Bee Gum Festival
October • 318.469.8498

Sulphur • Sulphur Heritage Festival
May • 800.456.7952 • visitlakecharles.org

Sulphur • Christmas
Under the Oaks Festival
December • 337.528.2270 • laffnet.org

Sunset • Herb and Garden Festival
May • 337.662.3542 • sunsetherbfestival.com

Thibodaux • Jubilee: A Festival of the Arts
• March • 985.448.4273 • nicholls.edu

Thibodaux • Louisiana
Swamp Stomp Festival
March • 985.448.4633 • visitlafourche.com

Thibodaux • Laurel Valley Spring Festival
April • 985.446.7456

Thibodaux • Firemen's Fair
May • 985.447.1986 • thibfiredept.org

Thibodaux • Let Freedom Ring Festival
July • 985-446-7218 • ci.thibodaux.la.us

Thibodaux • La Fete D'Ecologie
November • 800.259.0869 • neworleans.com

Thibodaux • Thibodeauxville Fall Festival
November • 985.446.1187
thibodauxchamber.com

Vidalia • Jim Bowie
BBQ Duel & Festival
September • 318.336.8223 • vidaliala.com

Ville Platte • Smoked Meat Festival
June • 337.363.6700
smokedmeatfestival.com

Ville Platte • Louisiana Cotton Festival
October • 337.363.6367
louisianacotton.com

Vinton • Spring Fest
& Civil War Reenactment
April • 800.456.7952 • visitlakecharles.org

Vinton • Vinton Heritage Festival
October • 800.456.7952 • visitlakecharles.org

Vivian • Louisiana Redbud Festival
March • 903.796.4781 • 318.375.3893
laredbud.com

Vivian • Country Christmas Festival
December • 318.375.5300

West Baton Rouge • Kite Fest Louisiana
April • 225.344.2920 • westbatonrouge.net

Westwego • Potpourri Festival
April • 504.341.9505

Westwego • Cypress Swamp Festival
November • 504.341.1003

Zachary • Zfest
March • 225.654.6777 • zfest.us

Zwolle • Loggers and Forestry Festival
May • 318.645.4307
zwolleloggersandforestryfestival.com

Zwolle • Zwolle Tamale Fiesta
October • 318.645.6141 318.645.2388
zwollela.net

Index

292 Recipes for 30 Varieties of Wild Game

The sportsman's outdoor experience doesn't end when the gun or the fishing gear has been put away. The challenge and reward of the quest are continued when the game is prepared into fabulous meals to be shared with friends and family.

Veteran hunter, fisherman, and chef Harold Webster delights sportsmen and those who cook game with seasonal recipes for venison, fish, fowl, and other delicacies from field and water. Fans of Webster's wild-game cookbooks and his popular newspaper column will recognize his trademark recipe clarity and his expert advice on handling, preparing, and serving game.

In addition to the recipes, Webster tells fascinating stories about the capturing, cleaning and cooking of the game. Stories like *Bow Season: Best Deer Hunt of the Year, Come Gather at Our Table, Stalking the Wild Fall Turkey,* **and** *Poochie was a Feist Dog* **make this book an entertaining read as well as an essential resource for creating memorable meals from any hunter's bounty.**

Game for All Seasons
$16.95 • 240 pp • 7 x 10
paperbound

Eat & Explore State Cookbook Series

Experience our United States like never before. Explore the distinct flavor of each state and discover their exceptional communities, beloved celebrations and remarkable destinations… all within the pages of this unique cookbook series. You'll enjoy favorite recipes straight from the kitchens of hometown cooks across the state. When dinner is done and everyone's ready to explore, this unique cookbook series offers even more. Each state's favorite events and destinations are profiled with everything you need to know to plan your trip. Eat & Explore State Cookbook Series offers family fun to suit every taste. Get started collecting the series today.

Now Available...

Eat & Explore Arkansas • 192 pages • 7 x 9
ISBN 978-1-934817-09-4 • $16.95

Eat & Explore Oklahoma • 268 pages • 7 x 9
ISBN 978-1-934817-11-7 • $16.95

Coming Soon...

Eat & Explore Minnesota • Summer 2012

Eat & Explore Virginia • Spring 2012

Eat & Explore Washington • Spring 2013

A Taste of America, One State at a Time
Collect them all!

Each title in the **HOMETOWN COOKBOOK SERIES** contains FAVORITE recipes from Hometowns all over the state plus fun side-bars featuring food festivals throughout the state. This series is great for anyone who loves to cook, cookbook collectors, and armchair travelers. $18.95 each.

If not available locally, use the order form below, or call us toll-free **1.888.854.5954**

or visit us on the web at

www.GreatAmericanPublishers.com

Order Form
mail to: Great American Publishers • P. O. Box 1305 • Kosciusko, MS 39090

❑ Check Enclosed

Charge to: ❑ Visa ❑ MC ❑ AmEx ❑ Disc

Card# _____

Exp Date _____ Signature _____

Name _____

Address _____

City _____ State _____ Zip _____

Phone_____

Email _____

Qty.	Title	Total
____	_____	_____
____	_____	_____
____	_____	_____
____	_____	_____
____	_____	_____
____	_____	_____
____	_____	_____

Subtotal _____
Postage ($3 first book; $.50 each additional) _____
Total _____